DUNCAN LONG

THE MINI-14

THE PLINKER, HUNTER, ASSAULT, AND EVERYTHING ELSE RIFLE

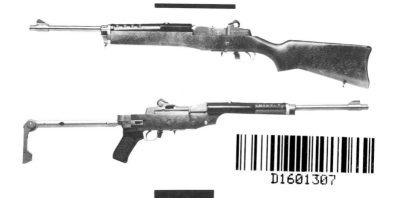

PALADIN PRESS
BOULDER, COLORADO

Also by Duncan Long:
AK47: The Complete Kalashnikov Family of Assault Rifles
The AR-15/M16: A Practical Guide
Assault Pistols, Rifles, and Submachine Guns
Combat Revolvers
The Complete AR-15/M16 Sourcebook: Revised and Updated
Homemade Ammo
Mini-14 Super Systems
Modern Combat Ammunition
Modern Sniper Rifles
Poor Man's Fort Knox
Ruger .22 Automatic Pistol: Standard/Mark I/Mark II Series
Streetsweepers: The Complete Book of Combat Shotguns
Super Shotguns
The Terrifying Three: Uzi, Ingram, and Intratec Weapons Families

The Mini-14: The Plinker, Hunter, Assault, and Everything Else Rifle
by Duncan Long

Copyright © 1987 by Duncan Long

ISBN 0-87364-407-7
Printed in the United States of America

Published by Paladin Press, a division of
Paladin Enterprises, Inc.
Gunbarrel Tech Center
7077 Winchester Circle
Boulder, Colorado 80301 USA
+1.303.443.7250

Direct inquiries and/or orders to the above address.

PALADIN, PALADIN PRESS, and the "horse head" design
are trademarks belonging to Paladin Enterprises and
registered in United States Patent and Trademark Office.

Visit our Web site at www.paladin-press.com

Contents

CHAPTER 1

History ... 1

CHAPTER 2

The Mini-14 Family of Rifles ... 23

CHAPTER 3

Care and Maintenance ... 41

CHAPTER 4

Accessories ... 65

APPENDIX

Manufacturers, Distributors, and Publishers ... 107

Warning

Technical data presented here, particularly technical data on ammunition and the use, adjustment, and alteration of firearms, inevitably reflects the author's individual beliefs and experience with particular firearms, equipment, and components under specific circumstances which the reader cannot exactly duplicate. The information in this book should therefore be used for guidance only and approached with great caution. Neither the author nor the publisher assume any responsibility for the use or misuse of information contained in this book.

Acknowledgments

Thanks are due to Sturm, Ruger and Company, Inc., who graciously loaned me several firearms to test during the writing of this book; and to the many, many companies that sent sample firearms, accessories, and products to inspect and test. Thanks also to the fine people at Paladin Press for making this book possible.

Thanks to my dad for his work in processing photos and a very special thanks to Maggie, Kristen, and Nicholas.

1.

History

When firearms are introduced to the public or the battlefield, they generally function poorly until the final design bugs are worked out. The Mini-14 is an exception to this rule; unlike the Garand, M-14, AR-15/M16, and other military-style rifles, it has always been known for reliable functioning and dependability.

There are several reasons for this. One is that the manufacturer, Sturm, Ruger and Company, took great pains to debug the weapon before offering it for sale. Another is that the Mini-14 is based on older, proven designs which have already undergone the problems associated with a new weapon. In effect, the Mini-14 was built on the historic precedents of previous designs.

MINI-14 PREDECESSORS

The "lineage" of the Mini-14 can be traced to the M1 Garand Rifle. The Garand Rifle was created by John Garand, in the course of sixteen years of work at the Springfield Armory. His rifle was adopted by the U.S. military in 1932 as the first semiautomatic rifle used by any military in the world. By 1941 most of the regular U.S.

troops carried the weapon and, after initial problems, it proved very reliable in combat. The Garand was improved as more guns were made, so that by 1945 General George Patton had written, "In my opinion, the M1 [Garand] is the greatest battle implement ever devised."

A huge number of the Garands were made. The United States had manufactured 5,500,000 when production finally ceased in the 1950s and a number of other countries made their own versions. Private firms in the U.S. are currently making the rifles as well.

Another important weapon to which the Mini-14 bears great resemblance is the M1 Carbine. This weapon was originally designed for troops who normally used the .45 pistol, but ended up being much more widely deployed. Since the carbine was designed as a pistol replacement, it was chambered for a rather anemic cartridge and was hurried into production with little testing and few modifications. With awkward field-stripping, poor location of the safety and magazine release, a fragile rear sight, and its poor cartridge, the M1 Carbine was less than ideal for combat.

Despite its shortcomings, the .30 Carbine became very popular because of its handy size and light weight. By the end of the Korean War, over six million had been made, more than any other small arm the U.S. has ever seen. Undoubtedly the M1 Carbine influenced military leaders and designers to try to create a lighter combat rifle in later years.

Another type of rifle that influenced the development of the Mini-14 dates back to German work done during World War II toward creating a small selective-fire rifle suited to actual combat conditions. While their weapon was heavy by modern standards, many consider it the first "assault rifle" (though the M1 Carbine is probably more deserving of the title). The German weapon was chambered for a small round and in 1943 was designated the *Maschinen Pistole*, or machine pistol, the designation used by the Germans for submachine guns. This rifle used sheet-metal stampings for the receiver and a detachable

The original rifle to which the "lineage" of the Mini-14 can be traced is the U.S. M1 Garand, created by John Garand. Various versions of the rifle include the standard M1 (top three rifles), and the rare M1-D sniper rifle (bottom of photo). Rifle second from the bottom is a standard M1 with a commercial scope mount which replaced the rear sight assembly. Photo courtesy of Springfield Armory, Inc.

30-round magazine and was simple to field-strip. It also had an unbelievable weight of 11.5 pounds!

The final rifle created by the German Nazi war effort became the *Sturmgewehr* (the MP43 and MP44 rifles) which was later designated the StG44. Unlike the M1 Carbine, no large numbers of the StG44 were ever created, though the basic design became the basis for the CETME and Heckler & Koch series of rifles and submachine guns.

The USSR also borrowed from both the German and U.S. designs to create the AK-47 and AKM rifles. For the USSR and its satellites, as well as many nonaligned nations and a few Western countries, the AK-47 design has been adopted with great success. This rifle borrows heavily from the German design concepts and, internally, from the Garand, with the AK bolt and trigger assemblies being near copies of the American weapon. Strange as it may seem, the AK firearms are in fact sister rifles to the Mini-14. While the AK rifles do have a number of improvements in the form of better control in automatic fire and simplified field-stripping, they also have some terrible design features, that fortunately were avoided in the Mini-14 design, like a safety that is hard and noisy to operate and rather excessive weight despite a short barrel.

By the 1950s, the U.S. weapons and parts inventory had become a resupplier's nightmare. Small arms in use included the M1 Garand, the M1 Carbine, the M3 "Grease Gun," the 1911-A1 pistol, and the Browning Automatic Rifle. Therefore, military planners felt a new firearm was needed to replace most of these weapons. The original "Army Ground Forces Equipment Review Board Preliminary Board Study" called for a selective-fire, 7-pound weapon using a .30-caliber round. The rifle that resulted from this study is of interest since it led, more or less, to the development of the Mini-14.

Unfortunately, developers of the rifle's cartridge ignored all military studies which showed that battle rifles from World War I through the Korean War had too much power for combat conditions. The U.S. Army created the T65 cartridge, a shortened version of the powerful, but out-

Inwardly the AK series of rifles have many parts copied from the Garand action, with the AK bolt and trigger assemblies being near copies of those of the American weapon. So, strange as it may seem, the AK series of firearms are, in fact, sister rifles to the Mini-14.

dated, .30-.06 round. The new round became the 7.62mm NATO/.308 Winchester, a powerful cartridge that made it impossible to create a lightweight rifle capable of effective automatic fire.

The rifle finally created for the new .308 cartridge was based on an experimental selective-fire Garand rifle designated the T20. The T20 rifle was nearly completed by the close of World War II but the project was terminated before production commenced. This design did, however, become the basis of the new military rifle as the old T20 was reworked at Springfield Armory by Lloyd Corbett. Major changes included a lighter barrel, addition of a 20-round detachable box magazine, changing the chamber for the light .308 Winchester/7.62mm round, and using a short-stroke gas system similar to that of the M1 Carbine. This modified T20 was redesignated the T44.

After a series of tests and improvements, the U.S. Army adopted two versions of the T44 in 1957. The T44E4 became the M14 rifle; the T44E5, a heavy-barreled version, became the M15 rifle. The M15 was never produced in any numbers because it lacked a quick-change barrel and was quite heavy.

The T44/M14 was too light for good control during automatic fire and the system itself was hard to make because of extremely close manufacturing tolerances. When it was finally fielded, the explosion of several rifles during training exercises coupled with problems of piston

The T44/M14 rifle is a modern version of the M14 made by Springfield Armory, Inc. Photo courtesy of Springfield Armory, Inc.

fouling blemished its image. When the design was finally debugged, many rifles were issued without the automatic-fire selector to keep the troops from using the hard-to-control automatic mode.

In an effort to make a weapon that could fire full-auto without loss of control, a pistol-grip stock with a forward grip was created and—with other minor changes—the new rifle was designated the M14E2. This later became the M14A1 in 1962 but, by then, the U.S. military had pretty well decided to go with the AR-15/M16 rifle with the more easily controlled .223 Remington round.

Even after the M16 was fielded, the M14 continued to be used as a sniper weapon. In this mode it is generally rebuilt, the barrel often glass bedded, and a Leatherwood auto-ranging scope mounted on it. A number of different stocks were made for the sniper rifles used during field tests in Vietnam. These included heavy recoil pads, pistol grips, and raised combs for use with the telescopic sight. The M14-based sniper rifle gained its M21 designation in 1975.

Shown is a modern civilian version of the M21. Photo courtesy of Springfield Armory, Inc.

A number of other variations of the M14 were also created for the national matches and NRA-sponsored shooting events. Several countries received M14s from the U.S. or manufactured the rifle themselves, so that many M14s are now available as surplus. Too, the company which purchased the Springfield Armory now manufactures its own version of the rifle, including a fully automatic M14, a semiauto M1A, the M1A-A1 (a short-barreled M1A, available with or without a folding stock), and the M14 (or M1A) decked out with the M14A1-style stock.

While the U.S. was experimenting with a variation of the Garand that later became the M14, Beretta of Italy was developing its own modified rifle as well. The Beretta plant had been manufacturing Garand rifles since the early 1950s, and it was only a matter of time before the innovative company started altering the basic, and somewhat outdated, design. The Beretta rifle was adopted by the Italian military in 1959 as the BM-59. The weapon differs slightly from the M14 but is basically identical to it in concept and execution except for the addition of short-barreled and folding-stock versions to the basic rifle models. A lightened semiauto version, the BM-62, was also created for the American civilian market. The privately-owned U.S. firm, Springfield Armory, purchased Beretta's inventory of BM-59 parts and is currently building semi-auto versions for the civilian market.

Modified Garand rifles are also sometimes seen on the civilian market, sometimes passed off as M14s. They are actually just M1 Garands with an added flash suppressor, with the forward upper band section removed to reveal the gas tube, and with a modification to allow them to be used with a 20-round magazine. These were "manufactured" commercially for a time as "MIIs" or as "M14 Garands" and not a few buyers have purchased one thinking they were getting a bona fide M14.

The Garand, M14, BM-59, and other Garand offspring all were good rifles, but they were heavy and fired a cartridge that was too powerful for combat. The stage had been set for the development of a smaller rifle based on

In Italy, Beretta altered the basic—and somewhat outdated—Garand design. The new Beretta rifle, adopted by the Italian military, was known as the BM-59. Shown is the BM-59 Alpine Rifle. Photo courtesy of Springfield Armory, Inc.

A number of different versions of the Beretta were manufactured for various countries outside Italy. Shown is the BM-59 Mark IV with its Nigerian stock. Note the similarity in concept to the "E2" stock used on the M14 rifle. Photo courtesy of Springfield Armory, Inc.

the Garand/M14 action in .223 or similar chambering.

Two such rifles were used during the trials for a replacement for the M14. One was made by Winchester and the other by Springfield Armory. Winchester's rifle looked very much like the selective-fire versions of the Mini-14 rifle; however, it had a rather flimsy rear sight and a hard-to-manufacture fluted barrel. Springfield Armory's .223 rifle resembled a scaled-down M14, including a gas tube which extended beyond the stock. Either of these rifles might well have become the new U.S. military weapon except that the third rifle used in the tests, the Armalite AR-15, had been developed well ahead of the others and, being well debugged, outshone both the Winchester and Springfield rifles in the tests.

Somewhat ironically, the Mini-14 (top) comes closer to satisfying both the original U.S. "Army Ground Forces Equipment Review Board Preliminary Board Study" than did the M14 (bottom)—except for the smaller caliber. The Mini-14 also comes closer to meeting the weight requirements for the current military rifle than does the M16A2 rifle.

STURM, RUGER & COMPANY, INC., THE EARLY YEARS

The Mini-14 was conceived by William Batterman Ruger, a man who has proven himself to be one of the major firearms designers of this century. Born in 1916 and raised in Brooklyn, New York, Ruger became interested in shooting and collecting firearms at an early age. After several attempts to gain employment with Colt Firearms and to sell a rifle design to Savage, Ruger ended up working in a North Carolina machine shop in the late 1930s.

Ruger's interest in firearms had led him to create several gun prototypes, including a machine gun in which the U.S. Army became interested. After turning down employment with Remington and Smith & Wesson, Ruger ended up at Springfield Armory in 1939 as a designer. He quickly became disillusioned with the work at Springfield and, after less than a year, was at work on his own back in North Carolina. There he made parts and created a working model of his own light machine gun design. After Ruger showed the new weapon to several manufacturers, Auto Ordnance Corporation hired him in 1941.

Auto Ordnance gave Ruger a shop and free reign to create experimental weapons; several of these machine guns were tested with others at the Aberdeen Proving Ground. Unfortunately, the U.S. military's requirements for a machine gun had changed just before the weapons were tested so that none of Ruger's guns were accepted! Both Ruger and Auto Ordnance apparently decided not to be burnt again, and discontinued work aimed at meeting the somewhat whimsical needs of the U.S. government.

Having all but given up on designing guns for profit, Ruger ended up machining parts and manufacturing hand tools in a small business he set up in Southport, Connecticut. Though the tools he produced were of high quality, sales apparently were not all that good since his products had to carry a higher price tag due to their quality. Unlike many, Ruger learned from his troubles and was soon to use his knowledge of how to set up and design manufacturing tools as well as how to produce products at competitive prices.

Fortunately, Ruger met a painter, Alexander M. Sturm, who was also a gun collector; they became close friends and Sturm became interested in a new pistol design Ruger had created. With Sturm putting up most of the money, the two men formed a company to manufacture the pistol. With the $50,000 they collected, Sturm and Ruger started business in 1949 with a small magazine ad and a favorable review of the new pistol in *American Rifleman.*

In 1949, the only target pistol that competed with the new Ruger pistol was the Colt Woodsman. Because of the use of a design that allowed production of the Ruger pistol at a lower price, the Ruger pistols sold at only $37.50 while the Colt pistols, which required a lot of machining, sold for $60 each. The orders for the Ruger pistol poured in and the new company became an overnight financial success. (Shortly after this, Sturm died; the pistol's heraldic falcon trademark on the pistols was changed from red to black to mark his death.)

In 1953, riding on a crest of orders for the pistol, Ruger took advantage of the cowboy/fast-draw craze and created an improved, updated version of the single-action revolver, first in .22 LR and later in a centerfire version. Unlike other single-action revolvers which were based on older Colt-style designs, the Ruger pistol was quite tough and could survive the abuse dealt out by quick-draw fans. As word of the Ruger pistol's toughness spread, it, too, was a huge success in the commercial marketplace and established a good base from which Ruger could market other firearms. By 1959, Ruger's company had to move into a larger building and, a year later, build an addition to the new building to make it fifty percent larger in order to handle the growing number of orders for the firearms they were building.

There are a number of reasons for Ruger's success. One is his excellent design know-how. This was coupled with his ability to discern what type of firearms would sell well in the U.S. market (Ruger has never used any market studies for any of his firearms). As the company grew, another reason for the company's success became apparent: Ruger had a knack for creating teams of workers capable of perfecting his designs and debugging new firearms before they were offered to the public.

The designs of Ruger's guns incorporate more than looks and function. They also take advantage of modern industrial methods so that, not only are they tough and attractive, they are also inexpensive to produce and can be offered at very competitive prices. Expensive milling operations are kept to a minimum while stampings and weldings—coupled with investment casting methods starting in the early 1960s—are used to create frames and other large parts.

In 1960, Ruger entered the rifle market with its .44 Magnum rifle which was a gas-operated rifle with a tubular magazine. The rifle was originally marketed under the "Deerstalker" label but this was dropped due to confusion with the "Deerslayer" shotgun being sold by Ithaca. Since that time, the rifle has been known simply as the "Ruger 44 Carbine."

The Ruger 44 combined the "feel" of the M1 Carbine with a stock reminiscent to that of the old Western saddle rifle. Using a powerful pistol cartridge, the .44 Magnum, the rifle had low recoil while being ideal for short-range hunting purposes. The Ruger 44 was followed by the 10/22 rifle in 1964 which was a .22 LR carbine holding 10 rounds of ammunition. Unlike many other .22s of the time, the 10/22 was capable of functioning reliably with a wide range of ammunition right out of the box and has since become a sort of standard against which other .22 rifles are judged. In style and concept, both of these lightweight rifles undoubtedly set the stage for the Mini-14.

By 1963, demand had become so great for Ruger's guns that a subsidiary company, Pine Tree Castings, was formed to principally handle investment castings for Sturm, Ruger. The Pine Tree plant opened in 1964 at Newport, New Hampshire, and has since become the largest producer in the U.S. of investment castings for firearms; Sturm, Ruger uses more castings in their firearms than the rest of the firearms industry combined.

Investment castings are important to the production of the Mini-14 since they allow the M14-style receiver and parts to be used without requiring a lot of machining for each of the parts. Machining is necessary only on surfaces which require very smooth surfaces and polishing can be carried out only by removing small amounts of surface metal. Investment-cast parts are as strong or stronger than all machined pieces and are much stronger than similar parts in many other rifles which are brazed together. Too, where machining operations often require building a special tool for each step of the machining, the castings are all done with the same basic setup with only the molds needing to be changed from one parts run to another. All of this gave Ruger a lot of room to design the rifle while keeping the price of the finished firearm at about half that of comparable machined weapons.

In 1967, taking another walk through the past and updating the firearm with commercial success, Ruger created his "Number One" rifle which was a single-shot rifle modeled after the Farquharson rifles of the late 1800s.

At this same time, Ruger worked toward introducing two models of a new "classic" car which he'd designed after the 1927 Bentley. Despite the excellent reviews the cars received, they were never actually marketed. (Apparently, meeting the demand for guns seemed to be as much as the company was willing to tackle at this point. Many are still holding their breath hoping that the cars will finally be marketed in the near future.)

The next year saw the introduction of a "classic" bolt-action rifle, the M-77. Again this rifle coupled the looks of older rifles with improved design to create competitively priced, reliable rifles. In the late 1960s when the M-77 was introduced, the fashion for rifles was lots of white spacers, Monte Carlo combs, and other bric-a-brac of nearly Baroque proportions. The M-77 wasn't burdened with any of these affectations. The M-77's functional design was received as a blow to many designers in the gun world and many shooters; sick of the ornate stocks of other companies they quickly purchased an M-77. And the rifle proved to be as reliable as its clean lines suggested.

In 1971, Ruger aimed for a slightly different market with the introduction of three double-action revolvers designed for law-enforcement/self-defense use. (As with the Mark I automatic pistol, over a million of these double-action revolvers had been sold 13 years later.) Another updated classic was released in 1972 in the form of a black powder "Old Army" single-action six shooter.

THE MINI-14

To make a long story short, 1972 saw the introduction of the Mini-14 after more than five years of engineering, testing, and development by Ruger and his staff. Initial sales were limited to government and law-enforcement agencies. In 1976, when the company had expanded its facilities and production was going smoothly, the non-selective-fire Mini-14 was offered for sale to the public.

Initially, Sturm, Ruger & Company, Inc., offered the rifles with only a five-shot box magazine, with 10- and 20-round magazines to be offered later on. These large-capacity magazines never became readily available outside the law-enforcement community, however, and a large market formed for large-capacity magazines manufactured by companies other than Ruger. (During the late 1970s, there was even one company that produced counterfeit 30-round magazines with a phony Ruger stamp and other trademarks! Because some of these magazines functioned poorly, some shooters thought there were problems with their rifles when, in fact, it was the boot-leg magazines that were faulty.)

Like other Ruger firearms, the Mini-14 proved to be a smashing success. By the mid-1980s, Ruger had to create a plant devoted just to Mini-14 manufacture. Many police units have found the rifle more useful than a shotgun since it has long-range accuracy and power with less penetration than larger-caliber rifles, especially when loaded with expanding bullets.

On the home front, many home owners like the idea of a "varmint" rifle that can double as a combat weapon if and when things go down the tubes; the rifle's "sporter" profile enabled those interested in self-defense to own a modern paramilitary rifle without raising the curiosity or fear that a military assault rifle normally stirs up.

Probably the final clincher for the Mini-14 was its price.

Shown is the paramilitary 20GB version of the Mini-14. Photo courtesy of Sturm, Ruger.

Because of the use of investment castings of the receiver and twenty-four other parts, the strong steel receiver was made with a minimum of machining. This gave it strength at a low price, and made the Mini-14 perfect for anyone on a limited budget.

As the rifle became popular, with over a million made by the late 1980s, a huge aftermarket business sprang up which offered a wealth of good—and not so good—accessories. A Mini-14 owner could customize his rifle to suit his needs for just a few more dollars; and while the total price of a heavily customized rifle might approach that of the off-the-rack military rifle, it could be quickly changed to serve several purposes or purchased in install-ments, the rifle first and the accessories later.

The Mini-14—equipped with accessories of various types—appealed to the serious shooter, the police, hunters, varminters, survivalists, and even the Walter Mittys. Sales of the rifles and accessories grew by leaps and bounds.

Added to the handiness of the rifle was its reliability. Mini-14s have gained a reputation for eating almost any

Shown is a standard series 181 Mini-14 which has been customized with the addition of an extended magazine, Choate ventilated hand-guard (which replaced the then-standard wooden handguard), Choate flash suppressor, and an Uncle Mike's sling.

type of properly sized ammunition. Ammunition too weak to cycle more expensive rifles can often be fired from the Mini-14 with no problems. The rifle has a 1-in-10 twist so that in addition to lightweight bullets, heavier bullets are also stabilized properly when fired. Having been designed with both the sporting and paramilitary markets in mind, the Mini-14 also uses the larger headspacing needed to chamber 5.56mm NATO rounds; unlike some sporters which can't safely handle military ammunition, the Mini-14 can handle virtually all types of .223/5.56mm ammunition. The only exception to this is reloaded ammunition that has not been properly full-case resized. Often such ammunition may not chamber reliably. Also, the Ruger Company cautions against the use of reloaded ammunition which doesn't use cannelured bullets since these bullets may create excessive pressures if they are pushed back into the cartridge during chambering.

Perhaps Ruger's most radical addition to the Mini-14 group would have been an upscaled version chambered for .308 Winchester. This rifle was called the XGI (which refers to the fact that it was quite similar to the original M14). The new rifle was made to be used with a scope and has a somewhat fragile flip-up rear sight for emergency use.

The XGI was scheduled for release late in 1985 or early in 1986, but it was delayed by a number of months because the company made some design changes, the most noticeable of which was the addition of a gas tube extension to the front of the stock, under the barrel; this was to act as a buffer to lower felt recoil somewhat, as well as to make the rifle function with a wide variety of ammunition.

Unfortunately, this work proved to be somewhat of a dead-end. While the new XGI design worked well with some ammunition, it didn't have the accuracy of the Mini-14 or other Sturm, Ruger products. Therefore, on August 6, 1986, the following press release was sent out by Ruger:

> Sturm, Ruger & Company will not manufacture or sell the Ruger XGI rifle as previously

The Rancher Rifle and the "discontinued" XGI both have integral scope ring mounts molded into their receivers (the half-moon areas to the front of the sight and above the charging handle).

The original XGI rifle is shown above. Photo courtesy of Sturm, Ruger.

The "improved" XGI functioned much more reliably than the original version of the rifle, which Ruger never released. Photo courtesy of Sturm, Ruger.

announced...

Reliability of function has been variable with the XGI rifle from the early pre-production prototypes. Extensive testing over an extended period of time with various modifications in the gas system and a series of design changes have only minimally improved the performance characteristics of the XGI...

Ruger has built its business and reputation on quality and we will only produce firearms that enhance this reputation.

Thus, after extensive research and pre-production costs, Sturm, Ruger abandoned the XGI rifle. A limited number of XGI rifles in .308 Winchester were produced but were used only in testing and evaluation work and none were ever sold to the general public.

The Mini-14 was designed to be light and handy, but there are some trade-offs to such a design. Its lightweight barrel can't be fired with water in it or used for a crowbar, nor can you drive a car over it and be sure of having a shootable firearm afterward! Likewise, the Mini-14 cannot digest 20,000 rounds during military training without showing some wear and tear. However, most owners are willing to baby the rifle a bit in exhange for a low price and lighter weight.

On both the civilian and the military market, two trends are apparent. One is the shortened rifle created by cutting the barrel down to 10 to 12 inches and/or adding a folding or telescoping stock. Sturm, Ruger itself offers several such models, and a wide range of aftermarket folding stocks are also available. While muzzle flash is greater, the weapon has more power than its pistol-cartridge-firing submachine gun counterpart. Such weapons are ideal for use by bodyguards or special police units.

The second trend is the "bullpup" design, which creates a light, short rifle *without* shortening the barrel to the point where it cuts down on the bullet's velocity or creates excessive muzzle noise and flash. This design places the

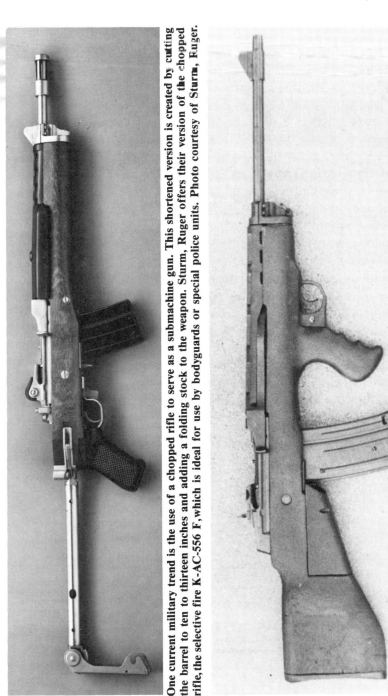

One current military trend is the use of a chopped rifle to serve as a submachine gun. This shortened version is created by cutting the barrel to ten to thirteen inches and adding a folding stock to the weapon. Sturm, Ruger offers their version of the chopped rifle, the selective fire K-AC-556 F, which is ideal for use by bodyguards or special police units. Photo courtesy of Sturm, Ruger.

The Mini-14 is ideally suited for bullpup use since its operating rod and recoil spring are located below the barrel and to the front of the receiver. Shown is a bullpup stock, based on the Westminister Arms stock, created by the author.

pistol grip ahead of the magazine and most of the mechanism of the receiver. The rear of the receiver becomes the butt of the stock. A bullpup-stocked rifle is shorter by the pull length—trigger to butt—of a regular stock.

The Mini-14's operating rod and recoil spring are located below the barrel and to the front of the receiver. This makes it simple to create a bullpup stock with little modification other than the addition of a higher sighting system and a trigger-rod extension system. A few companies already offer bullpup kits and, while it is doubtful that public demand will cause Ruger to create such a configuration, it is always possible that Sturm, Ruger might even offer such a rifle in the future.

While military weapons may move on to caseless ammunition and exotic mechanisms and sighting systems, the Mini-14 will undoubtedly remain a favorite among hunters and varminters, the law-enforcement community, and those wanting an unobtrusive combat rifle—at least until Ruger brings another idea off the drawing board to replace it. Until that time, Mini-14 sales in the U.S. will probably continue to be the highest of any centerfire rifle manufactured.

2.

The Mini-14 Family of Rifles

A lot more work went into the design of the Mini-14 than many suppose. An exact ratio can't be drawn from the M14 to the other rifles since both weapons must be scaled both for the user and the smaller cartridge. Too, the .223/5.56mm cartridge has a high-pressure range, so that many Mini-14 parts have to remain nearly as large as those of the M14 to keep them from breaking over time. In fact, some parts of the Mini-14 are actually larger than those of the M14 to avoid some of the larger rifle's problems with part breakage. (Thus, the idea of somehow simply shrinking the M14 design to get a Mini-14 is only practical for those who daydream about such things.)

The Mini-14 also was designed to be manufactured by investment casting and stamped-metal fabrication rather than costly machining and has a number of design modifications to accommodate this manufacturing process.

The M14 had a number of problems with its gas-operating rod; even some of the newest M14s can be damaged by firing commercial ammunition loaded with heavy bullets. To avoid this problem, Ruger more or less reversed the M14 gas piston system. In the M14, the gas piston enters a fixed cylinder; on the Mini-14, the gas piston is hollow and fits over a stationary gas nozzle connected to the barrel. Besides allowing for a heavier piston that is nearly impossible to bend or damage, the system also can go longer without becoming fouled and reduces felt recoil somewhat.

Another interesting design change for the Mini-14 is found in the trigger group. Ruger apparently studied the original source of the design that Garand had adapted to his rifle, the Browning/Remington Model 8/81 rifles. Thus, the Mini-14 has a common-ancestor relationship with the Garand and M14 rather than being an offspring.

The original M14 stock tends to crack or char, despite its heavy design, with extended firing. Ruger therefore beefed up the forward stock/gas port area and lined it with a steel plate, placed the gas tube inside the stock, increased the magazine-well reinforcement, and changed the overall lines of the stock somewhat. For aesthetic reasons, the butt got the classic Ruger look of an 1800s rifle stock.

Ruger wisely did little to change the Garand and M14 designs that worked well other than to scale and adapt them to the Mini-14. The safety, magazine, and magazine release are all more or less copies of the original. As with the M14, the Mini-14's safety is located inside the trigger guard and can be put on "safe" before cycling the bolt—a good safety feature. The magazine release is just behind the magazine well. This type of safety and magazine release make the rifle convenient for both left- and right-handed shooters. The reciprocating charging handle located on the right of the rifle's receiver also does away with the need for a forward assist; this cuts down on a number of parts and also makes the rifle easier to use.

The trigger pull on the Mini-14 is ideal for precision shooting. It is set at the factory to "break" at 4½ pounds and can be lightened by a good gunsmith.

On selective-fire models, the selector is located on the right side of the receiver above the trigger at the stock/receiver line. Ruger automatic rifles have two modes: full auto and the more practical three-round burst. The built-in safety feature of all Mini-14s keeps the firing pin in a retracted position until the bolt is locked; this makes the rifle very safe to use, as the firing pin cannot fire a cartridge with the bolt unlocked.

On current-production Mini-14s, the bolt hold-open device locks the action open following the last shot. This should not be used as a safety, since it can easily be jarred loose, but it is very handy when cleaning the rifle and promotes fast reloading. The hold-open mechanism can be engaged by either an empty magazine or with the small bolt-lock plunger located on the top left edge of the receiver just ahead of the sight.

There are several series of rifles in the Mini-14 family. Early production models were in the 180 series denoted by the "180" prefix in the serial number. These have a slightly different design and specifications from later models. The most noticeable internal difference is a thinner gas piston. Externally, some of the earliest 180-series rifles have a rear sight that is finger adjustable with knobs on the left and right rather than on the left and top of the receiver as with modern standard Mini-14s. Most 180-series rifles also use a flat piece of stamped metal for the forward sling swivel rather than a piece of formed wire. All 180-series rifles also have an external bolt hold-open mechanism which has proven prone to jamming in a dirty environment; the bolt-lock cover plate is also missing on the 180 series; instead the left side of the upper receiver is solid. Because some of the differences make the 180 series slightly less reliable than other Mini-14s, and because the 180 series can't use many accessories designed for later series, it would be wise to leave the 180-series rifles to the collector.

In 1977, the 181 series of the Mini-14 more or less did away with the 180's problems by changing the rear sight, enlarging the gas piston and magazine release, and enclosing the bolt hold-open mechanism inside the receiver. The 182 series introduced in 1980 was nearly identical to the 181 but was made of non-reflective, satin finish stainless steel.

A few receivers on the early stainless steel Mini-14s were heat-treated incorrectly and were excessively hard as a result. These rifles had serial numbers below 182-51929 and only one proof mark. The Ruger factory will replace or retreat these weapons if they are returned to the company. Once this work is done, a second proof mark is placed on the rifle. Therefore, when purchasing a stainless steel Mini-14, it is wise first to check the serial number. If it is in the group below 182-51929, look for two proof marks. The Sturm, Ruger proof mark consists of a stylized "R" in a circle.

The stainless steel Mini-14s are highly resistant to corrosion, making them ideal for environments which might quickly wreck blued-steel weapons. As stainless steel retains heat to a greater extent than does regular steel, the stainless steel barrels are apt to overheat with excessive firing, especially in the automatic mode. This may be a consideration for some users.

The rear sight on the 181/182 series uses both elevation and windage wheels. The elevation adjustment wheel is in front of the peep sight and the windage adjustment knob is on the left side of the rear sight assembly. Both knobs are locked in place by a detent and can be adjusted only when the tip of a bullet or other small tool depresses the release. One click changes the point of impact 1.5 inches at 100 yards. The zero can't be thrown off accidentally during heavy use—such as in combat. Mini-14s are sighted in during final testing at the factory and will generally be nearly zeroed out of the box with most commercial ammunition.

The front sights of the commercial models are a single blade that appears fragile since it lacks the protective dog ears common on most military rifles. In fact, the dog ears are unnecessary due to the size and length of the blade and because the sighting adjustments are made on the rear sight. If the front sight is ever damaged to the point that it is out of alignment, chances are that the barrel will also be damaged beyond use. Paramilitary models usually have a front sight with dog ears similar to that of the M14 or other military rifles.

In 1982, Ruger introduced the "Ranch Rifle," denoted by a 187 serial-number prefix. This rifle has a flip-up rear sight, scope ring mounting lugs cut into the receiver (rings are included), a buffer system that reduces recoil, and a stationary ejector, mounted to the inside of the receiver, which propels spent cases to the side so that they won't hit the scope. Sturm, Ruger manuals caution shooters to stay clear of the ejection port and suggest not firing the rifle with the left-hand hold since the cartridges are often hurled out with enough force to create an injury. The butt stock of the Ranch Rifle also departs from the Ruger look somewhat.

From about the mid-1980s on, all Mini-14 rifles have had a ventilated plastic handguard with aluminum insert rather than the earlier wooden upper handguard.

Several other chamberings are available for the Ranch Rifle. A few were chambered in .222 Remington; these were originally made for export; few were sold in the U.S. Late in 1986, Ranch Rifles should be available in 7.62 × 39mm chambering; this will allow shooters the option of using a Mini-14 for some types of hunting not normally done with the .223. This version is called the "Mini-30."

Because of the width of the 7.62 × 39mm cartridge, the Ranch Rifle receiver will be wider in the 7.62 × 39mm; eventually, the .223 Ranch Rifle receiver will also be widened so that the same receivers can be used on either rifle.

After nearly a year's delay, plans for producing the XGI rifle were finally dropped in August 1986. This sister rifle to the Mini-14 would have brought the Ruger rifles full circle since it was chambered for .308 Winchester of the original M14 that the Mini-14 was modeled after. However, unlike the Mini-14, the XGI was unable to better the original M14 design.

Except for a rubber recoil pad and slightly larger dimensions in some areas, the XGI resembled the Mini-14/5R right down to its flip-up rear sight and integral scope mount. The initial XGI was to be chambered for .308 Win-

The front sights of commercial models of the Mini-14 are comprised of a single blade that appears fragile but is in fact strong due to its size and length.

chester (7.62mm NATO) with a model chambered in .243 Winchester slated for release a half year later. If these had met with success, it would have been probable that more chamberings and stainless steel versions would also have been developed.

The original version of the XGI which first came to public attention as a prototype version in 1985 had its gas port encased in the stock; few if any of these were discovered in the design and the rifle's release delayed. The "improved" version of the XGI had an exposed section of the gas tube ahead of the fore grip. The extension apparently was to act as a gas buffer and apparently improve the performance of the XGI with a variety of ammunition. At this point, Sturm, Ruger felt that the "bugs" in the XGI had been overcome; further testing proved that the rifle still didn't have the accuracy needed for a hunting rifle, however, so the company finally decided not to go into production with the XGI rifle.

The rear sight on the Ranch Rifle models of the Mini-14 (and the XGI prototype rifles) is slightly different from those of the standard Mini-14 rear sights. While still a "peep" sight, it flips down out of the way when the scope is being used. This makes it possible to have a much lower scope mount so that the cheek weld is simple to maintain whether using a scope or the sight. The only drawback to the design is that the rear sight is rather fragile when

In the up position. Windage is adjusted on the Ranch Rifle model with a small hex wrench while the elevation is adjusted—somewhat awkwardly—by loosening two small screws on either side of the peep hole. It should also be noted that when aftermarket stocks, which are longer than the Ruger stock, are mounted on the Ranch Rifle, proper scope mounting is difficult to achieve with some scopes because the Ruger-ring mount system limits the rearward distance a scope can be mounted to. When using an extended, aftermarket stock, a scope with extended eye relief should be mounted on the rifle.

There are three basic models of the Mini-14: a semiauto sporting version (the Mini-14/5 and the Mini-14/5R Ranch Rifle); the police/military Mini-14/20GB with bayonet lug and flash suppressor; and the AC-556 selective-fire version—with the three-round burst capability in addition to semiauto and full-auto fire. Within these three model groupings, the rifles are offered by Ruger with different barrel lengths, magazine capacity, folding/stationary stock choices, and the choice of stainless steel or standard blued steel finishes.

Current production Mini-14 rifles have an aluminum-lined plastic handguard which helps prevent overheating and protects the hand from the operating rod during firing.

Generally, the Ruger Company denotes the various models and variants of its weapons in the following ways: stainless steel parts are denoted by a "K" prefix; folding stocks with an "F" prefix; 5-round magazines with a "5" suffix; 20-round magazines with a "20" suffix; flash suppressor/grenade launcher/bayonet lugs with a "GB" suffix; and scope mounts milled into the top of the receiver for scope rings with an "R" suffix.

So, with the three basic series, three models, and the various options, the following rifles are readily available from Sturm, Ruger & Company, Inc.:

1. The Mini-14/5, semiauto with a blued finish and a 5-round magazine.
2. The Mini-14/5R or Ranch Rifle, semiauto with a blued finish and a standard 5-round magazine, scope mount, and special Ruger scope rings.
3. The Mini-14/5R-F which, at the time of this writing, isn't available but will probably soon be introduced. If so, it would be the Ranch Rifle with a blued finish, standard 5-round magazine, scope mount, special Ruger scope rings, and folding stock.
4. The K Mini-14/5R, the stainless steel version of the Ranch Rifle with standard 5-round magazine, scope mount, and special Ruger scope rings (available in .223 and 7.62 × 39mm).
5. The K Mini-14/5R-F, the semiauto Ranch Rifle in stainless steel with a folding stock and 5-round magazine, scope mount, and special Ruger scope rings (available in .223 and 7.62 × 39mm).
6. The Mini-14/5-F, the standard semiauto, blued rifle with the 5-round magazine and Ruger folding stock.
7. The K Mini-14/5, the semiauto, stainless steel rifle with 5-round magazine.
8. The K Mini-14/5-F, the semiauto, stainless steel rifle with standard 5-round magazine and folding stock.
9. The Mini-14/20GB, the paramilitary semiauto blued rifle with standard 5-round magazine and folding stock.
10. The Mini-14/20GB-F paramilitary semiauto blued rifle with bayonet lug, flash suppressor, 20-round magazine, and folding stock.
11. The K-Mini-14/20GB semiauto stainless steel rifle with bayonet lug, 20-round magazine, and flash

suppressor.

12. The K-Mini-14/20GB-F semiauto stainless steel rifle with bayonet lug, flash suppressor, 20-round magazine, and folding stock.

13. The AC-556, blued selective-fire rifle with 18-inch barrel, flash suppressor, and bayonet lug.

14. The AC-556 F blued, selective-fire rifle with folding stock and usually a 13-inch barrel with flash suppressor but without bayonet lug.

15. The K-AC-556 stainless steel, selective-fire rifle with 18-inch barrel, bayonet lug, and flash suppressor.

16. The K-AC-556 F stainless steel, selective-fire rifle with folding stock and usually a 13-inch barrel with flash suppressor.

Current production Mini-14/5 rifles have an aluminum-lined plastic handguard; those first sold had a wooden handguard. Photo courtesy of Sturm, Ruger.

The Mini-14/5R or Ranch Rifle, is available in .223 and 7.26 × 39mm; a few were also made in .222. Photo courtesy of Sturm, Ruger.

The Mini-14/5R (top) or Ranch Rifle, with the rear sight flipped down and a scope mounted, has special Ruger scope rings which allow the scope to be placed directly on the receiver of the rifle. The K Mini-14/5R (middle) is the stainless steel version of the Ranch Rifle with standard 5-round magazine, scope mount and special Ruger scope rings. The K Mini-14/5R-F (bottom) is the semiauto Ranch Rifle in stainless steel with a folding stock and a standard 5-round magazine, scope mount, and special Ruger scope rings. Both rifles are available in .223 and 7.62 × 39mm. Photos courtesy of Sturm, Ruger.

The K Mini-14/5 (top) is the semiauto, stainless steel version of the Mini-14 181 series, and is identical to the blued edition except for the steel used in its manufacture. Note that the 5-round magazine does not extend below the stock line. The K Mini-14/5-F (bottom) is a semiauto, stainless steel rifle with a standard 5-round magazine, and a folding stock—shown extended. The wooden stock has a plastic grip; in this form this rifle was once restricted to military and police sales, but is now available to the general public. Photos courtesy of Sturm, Ruger.

The Mini-14/20GB (top) is a paramilitary semiauto blued rifle with a bayonet lug, flash suppressor, and 30-round magazine. The Mini-14/20GB-F shown is basically identical to the Mini-14/20GB, except that it is equipped with the folding stock and a 20-round magazine. Photos courtesy of Sturm, Ruger.

The Mini-14/20GB-F is presented (top) with its folding stock folded. The AC-556 (bottom) is a blued selective-fire rifle with 18-inch barrel, flash suppressor, and bayonet lug, and has a selector at the right rear of the receiver above the trigger. Photos courtesy of Sturm, Ruger.

The AC-556 F is a blued, selective-fire rifle with folding stock and a 13-inch barrel with flash suppressor, with no bayonet lug. Photo courtesy of Sturm, Ruger.

The K-AC-556 F is a stainless steel, selective-fire rifle with folding stock, and usually a 13-inch barrel with flash suppressor. The stock is shown folded (top) and extended (bottom). Photos courtesy of Sturm, Ruger.

A number of other versions are possible, including grenade launcher/bayonet mounts on various versions, 20-round magazines with the standard version, or shorter barrels on the standard and GB versions.

Because the location of the safety, magazine release, etc., are identical on all Mini-14s (and the M14 variants offered by other companies), the rifles are ideal for shooters who need to switch calibers. As many hunters and soldiers have discovered that firing different types of weapons during moments of stress can be made easier if all weapons are operated in an identical fashion, having different positions for safeties, charging levers, or magazine releases can cause failure when the heat is on. For hunters, special police units, or soldiers, the Mini-14 rifles are ideally suited for a variety of uses.

An extensive family of weapons can be created from the Mini-14 and similar weapons. With the Mini-14 (perhaps in several calibers such as the .223, 7.62 × 39mm, and —with a .22 conversion unit— .22 LR) and a modern M14 varient in .308 (or a Garand in .30-.06), it's possible to have a family of rifles similar to those created by Heckler & Koch (HK-91/93/94, etc.), the Stoner weapons system, or the AR-15/AR-10. Unlike these other families which have failed to catch on, the Mini-14/M14 family can be easily purchased and costs considerably less than its often expensive paramilitary counterparts. So, for relatively little money, a firearms enthusiast can own a family of rifles capable of fulfilling a wide variety of hunting or combat roles. Springfield Armory offers the widest choice of variations and models of the M14 and Garand rifles; they have modified the basic M14 design so that the rifle is stronger and more reliable than those made for military users.

It is probable that other variations of the Mini-14 will be marketed by Ruger in the near future. In the decades ahead, when the Mini-14 patent rights have run out, it is also probable that other companies will start manufacturing the rifle. Although early Sturm, Ruger & Company literature called the Mini-14 "the world's most expensive plinker," a lot of people have found the rifle to be both inexpensive and a most useful tool. It is doubtful that this will change in the near future.

MINI-14/5, MINI-14/5R Specifications

Barrel length . . . . 18.5 in.
Caliber . . . . .223 Remington
Cyclic rate (approx.) . . . . 750 rpm
Length (approx.) . . . . 37.3 in.
Magazine (standard) 5-round
Muzzle velocity (approx.) . . . . 3,300 fps
Rifling . . . . 6 grooves, 1-in-10 or (in newer guns)
1-in-7, right-hand twist
Weight (approx.) . . . . 6.4 lbs.

MINI-14/20 GB Specifications

Barrel length . . . . 18.5 in.
Caliber . . . . .223 Remington
Cyclic rate (approx.) . . . . 750 rpm
Length (approx.) . . . . 37.3 in.
Magazine (standard) 20-round
Muzzle velocity (approx.) . . . . 3,300 fps
Rifling . . . . 6 grooves, 1-in-10, right-hand twist
Weight (approx.) . . . . 6.4 lbs.

AC-556 F Specifications

Barrel length . . . . 13 in.
Caliber . . . . .223 Remington
Cyclic rate (approx.) . . . . 750 rpm
Length (approx.) . . . . 33.5 in.
Length (stock folded) . . . . 23.8 in.
Magazine (standard) 20-round
Muzzle velocity (approx.) . . . . 3,000 fps
Rifling . . . . 6 grooves, 1-in-10, right-hand twist
Weight (approx.) . . . . 7.9 lbs.

XGI (Prototype) Specifications
Barrel length............................... 20 in.
Caliber .... .308 Winchester (7.62mm NATO)
Length (approx.)......................... 39.9 in.
Magazine (standard) 5-round
Muzzle velocity (approx.) .... (.308) 2,800 fps
Rifling .... 6 grooves, 1-in-10, right-hand twist
Weight (approx.)............................ 8 lbs.

M14 Specifications
Barrel length............................... 22 in.
Caliber .... .308 Winchester (7.62mm NATO)
Cyclic rate (approx.)..................... 750 rpm
Length (approx.) .... 44 in.
Magazine (standard) 20-round
Muzzle velocity (approx.)................ 2,800 fps
Rifling .... 4 grooves, right-hand twist
Weight (approx.) .... 9.6 lbs.

M14A1 Specifications
Barrel length............................... 22 in.
Caliber .... .308 Winchester (7.62mm NATO)
Cyclic rate (approx.)..................... 750 rpm
Length (approx.) .... 44 in.
Magazine (standard) 20-round
Muzzle velocity (approx.)................ 2,800 fps
Rifling .... 4 grooves, right-hand twist
Weight (approx.) .... 12.8 lbs.

3.

Care and Maintenance

A little care and know-how will greatly extend the life of a Mini-14; a neglected weapon will have a very short useful life. If you are careful, your Mini-14 can last a lifetime.

CLEANING

Many rifles and pistols have had their accuracy ruined by improper cleaning. It's better not to clean a rifle's bore at all than to do a sloppy job.

To clean the bore properly, care must be taken not to damage the muzzle end of the rifling. The cleaning rod must not rub against the bore. Because the Mini-14 must be cleaned from the muzzle, be especially careful with the cleaning rod. Aluminum cleaning rods should be avoided if possible or kept religiously clean to keep them from picking up bits of grit which can cut into the metal of the bore during cleaning. U.S. military surplus steel rods are much better for cleaning the bore. A good source for these rods is Sierra Supply (see the appendix).

Break-Free CLP is probably the best lubricant and cleaner for the Mini-14. This material was created for U.S.

military rifles and can be used over a wide temperature range; another real plus is that Break-Free does away with having to use both a bore cleaner and oil; Break-Free cleans and lubricates. Whenever possible, let the rifle sit for half an hour or so after applying Break-Free since it takes a while to set up and offer its full lubrication. Break-Free is also available from Sierra Supply.

Birchwood Casey makes several good products for gun maintenance. Their "Sheath" anti-rust cloth works well and is ideal for the once-a-year massive cleaning that most guns get. They also make products to help clean and maintain wood stocks. Birchwood Casey products are available at most gun stores.

When you've finished cleaning the rifle, check the bore to be sure it is clear of patch threads and oil. Any material left in the barrel can ruin it with one shot.

Don't oil the gas tube or inside the piston. Oil in these areas can char and damage the assembly or cause poor functioning. Avoid getting oil on wooden stocks as it can stain the wood or even damage it. Take care also not to leave oil in the magazine or chamber, where it can deactivate ammunition or create excessive chamber pressure since the oil will keep the brass cartridge from sealing the chamber properly when it is fired.

A light coating of oil is of use on the inside and outside of blued steel Mini-14s to help prevent the development of rust. Don't use too much oil on internal parts; it doesn't improve the lubricating properties and may actually gum things up as dirt is trapped in the oil. Use only light coats of lubricant on the Mini-14; too much oil will actually increase wear and tear.

Stainless steel is not really stainless but is certainly more resistant to corrosion that is blued steel. Stainless still needs to be cared for; a light coating of Break-Free and a good cleaning occasionally is in order. Some users have found that a light coat of car paste wax on the outside of a stainless steel firearm greatly improves its resistance to staining and lowers maintenance needs. If minor discoloration occurs on the surface of stainless steel, it can be buffed off with an ink eraser or metal-polishing compound. Use only light pressure when buffing the metal and take care to remove any grit left behind after you're done.

One real plus of the Ruger stainless steel rifles is that the internal parts (unlike stainless steel firearms made by other manufacturers) are made of stainless steel. This means the whole gun, not just the external parts, is corrosion resistant.

If you're storing your Mini-14 for several months or more, be sure it is not placed in a leather or plastic container which will collect moisture inside itself. Such a container will ruin a rifle in short order. When a rifle is stored away in a suitable container, be sure to clean it at least twice a year, more often if you live in an area of high humidity. Use a cloth with oil on it to lightly wipe all fingerprints off the surface of the metal so that it won't cause rust spots.

Touch-up blue is useful for keeping the finish on blued rifles looking new. Touch-up blue can also get a seller a better price on his rifle by making it look as good outside as it is inside. Minor rusting can also be removed from a blued rifle and the surface refinished with touch-up blue. A small rust spot can usually be removed by sanding it lightly with a very fine steel wool; touch-up blue is then used according to the instructions on the bottle. Lightly oil surfaces that have been touched up to prevent new rust spots from forming. Touch-up blue is available at most gun stores.

The barrel life of the Mini-14, especially on the stainless steel models, will be greatly shortened if long strings of shots are fired through the firearm without letting the barrel cool off. While this isn't normally a concern, it should be kept in mind for those doing a lot of combat-style practice.

TOOLS

The Mini-14 doesn't require many special tools to work

on or maintain it. A rear sight tool is useful for target shooting to adjust for windage. Parellex currently sells this tool.

A good drift punch or two and a rawhide mallet are quite useful as are needle-nosed pliers and a good set of screwdrivers.

When working on a firearm, try to create a soft surface on the work bench so that the rifle doesn't become scratched. It is also wise to place small parts in a container during disassembly. Ice cube trays, egg cartons, or similar containers work well.

FIELD-STRIPPING

While the field-stripping procedure (see exploded diagrams) for the various Mini-14 (and M14) rifles is nearly identical and complex, the procedure also gives greater access to many of the parts so that the Ruger rifles can be cleaned more thoroughly and completely.

Field-stripping is as follows:

1) Cycle the weapon to be sure it's empty and remove the magazine. The safety must be put into the "safe" position inside the trigger guard and the hammer cocked before field-stripping can commence.

2) Grasp the rear of the trigger guard and pull it forward and away from the rifle (a small punch or other tool can be placed in the hole at the rear of the trigger guard to aid in this task). This will allow the trigger group to be removed and free the barrel/receiver assembly.

3) If the stock (1-3) doesn't readily separate itself from the barrel and receiver, push the receiver forward while pulling up slightly. This should free it. Though not necessary for field-stripping, the upper handguard half (1-1) can be removed by pulling the rear end of the handguard away from the barrel to release its clip fastener. The rear of the handguard should be lifted up and then back to complete its removal.

4) On weapons with automatic-fire capabilities, it's

necessary to remove the trip lever/connector assembly on the right side of the receiver, just below the charging lever (2-1). This is done with the bolt closed by pushing the connector forward until it can be rotated clockwise. When the elongated hole in the connector assembly is aligned with the elongated stud on the sear release, lower the front end of the connector and the rear end of the lever can be lifted off the elongated stud of the sear release.

5) Place the barrel/receiver group upside-down on a flat surface. Push forward on the recoil spring guide (2-11) and the recoil spring (2-12) slightly to free them and then lift them out of the assembly (careful: these parts are under a great deal of spring tension). On the Ranch Rifle, the buffer bushing (3-15) and its cross pin (3-17) should also be removed at this point so that they don't fall out and become lost during cleaning.

6) Turn the receiver (3-16) rightside-up and pull the charging lever (2-1) toward the rear of the receiver until the locking projections on the slide line up with the disassembly notch on the right side of the receiver. Rotate the charging lever assembly down and outward to free it, then pull it to the rear to disengage it from the receiver.

7) Push the bolt assembly (4-1 through 4-7) forward and pivot it out toward the ejection port to remove it.

Normal maintenance and lubrication can be accomplished with only this much disassembly. Reassembly is basically a reversal of the above procedure. The safety must be engaged and the hammer cocked before the trigger assembly can be replaced into the rifle.

With Ranch Rifle (Mini-14/5R) models, it is best to remove the bolt hold-open assembly to reassemble. To remove the hold-open assembly, lightly tap at the top of the cover plate (3-21) on the left of the receiver. When the plate is removed, depress the plunger (3-8) and pull the bolt stop out (3-18) to the left of the receiver (through the opening created by the removal of the plate). Slowly remove the bolt stop plunger and its spring (3-11) from the top of the receiver. Now the bolt can be placed into the receiver; once that's done, replace the hold-open assembly. On most Ranch Rifles, the bolt can be replaced without removing the receiver plate by tilting the barrel up and placing the bolt into place with the rear projection of the firing pin extended back and lined up with the cut for it in the lower receiver bridge. As the bolt is pushed back with a wiggling motion, push down on the hold-open button several times until the bolt squeaks through. However, most users will find it easier to remove the plate and hold-open/ejector assembly.

Magazines can be taken apart by sliding out their base plates and easing out the spring and follower. Occasionally clean out magazines and *very lightly* lubricate the spring and other metal parts. Keep in mind that oil can deactivate ammunition.

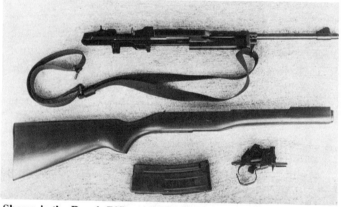

Shown is the Ranch Rifle with Uncle Mike's quick adjust sling and a Ram-Line 30-round Combo Magazine.

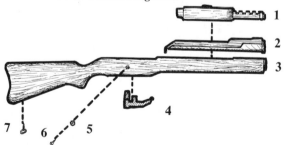

DIAGRAM ONE—STOCK ASSEMBLY. 1-1: Upper handguard half; 1-2: forearm liner; 1-3: stock; 1-4 stock reinforcement insert; 1-5: stock screw washer; 1-6: stock screw; 1-7: rear sling swivel.

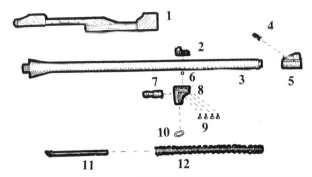

DIAGRAM TWO—CHARGING HANDLE/BARREL/RECOIL SPRING ASSEMBLIES. 2–1: Charging lever; 2–2: upper gas block; 2–3: barrel; 2–4: front sight roll pin; 2–5: front sight; 2–6: gas port bushing; 2–7: gas tube; 2–8: lower gas block; 2–9: gas block screws; 2–10: front sling swivel; 2–11: recoil spring guide; 2–12: recoil spring.

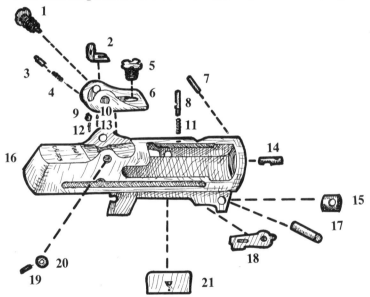

DIAGRAM THREE—RECEIVER ASSEMBLY. 3–1: Windage knob; 3–2: peep sight; 3–3: rear sight windage detent plunger; 3–4: rear sight windage detent plunger spring; 3–5: rear sight elevation adjustment knob; 3–6: rear sight base; 3–7: magazine catch retaining pin; 3–8: bolt lock plunger; 3–9: rear sight elevation detent plunger; 3–10: elevation plunger; 3–11: bolt stop spring; 3–12: rear sight elevation detent plunger spring; 3–13: elevation plunger spring; 3–14: magazine catch; 3–15: buffer bushing (found only on Ranch Rifle version of the Mini-14); 3–16: receiver; 3–17: barrel bushing cross pin (found only on Ranch Rifle); 3–18: bolt stop; 3–19: rear sight windage pin; 3–20: rear sight nut; 3–21: bolt lock cover plate.

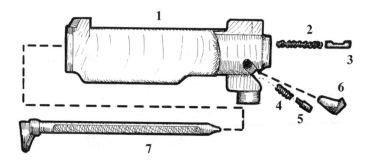

DIAGRAM FOUR—BOLT ASSEMBLY. 4–1: Bolt; **4–2:** ejector spring (not found on Ranch Rifle); **4–3:** ejector (not found on Ranch Rifle); **4–4:** extractor plunger spring; **4–5:** extractor plunger; **4–6:** extractor; **4–7:** firing pin.

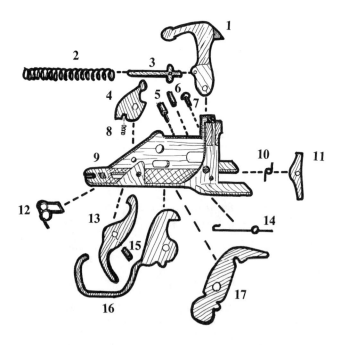

DIAGRAM FIVE—TRIGGER ASSEMBLY. 5–1: Hammer; **5–2:** hammer spring; **5–3:** hammer strut; **5–4:** secondary sear; **5–5:** safety spring retaining pin; **5–6:** hammer pivot pin; **5–7:** magazine latch pivot pin; **5–8:** secondary sear spring; **5–9:** trigger housing; **5–10:** magazine release lever spring; **5–11:** magazine release lever; **5–12:** trigger spring; **5–13:** trigger; **5–14:** safety spring; **5–15:** trigger pivot pin; **5–16:** trigger guard; **5–17:** safety.

TUNING

Because the Mini-14 is designed to be lightweight, its accuracy is not as great as that of some heavier rifles. With standard FMJ (full metal jacket) ammunition, groups of three to five inches are to be expected at 100 yards, while quality ammunition with hollow-point bullets may give 2.5- to 3-inch groups at 100 yards. This is sufficient for most shooters and in fact offers greater accuracy than many owners are capable of obtaining.

Occasionally a Mini-14 seems to be plagued with less than ideal accuracy. While this may not be much of a problem in combat, it can be an aggravation on the target range or when hunting. Provided the barrel hasn't been damaged by improper cleaning or the like, inaccuracy problems usually are caused by a poor stock-to-barrel fit. Replacing the stock with one of the new plastic ones often improves the shot grouping. Many shooters have found groups reduced by half when they've added a plastic Choate stock to their rifles.

For those who wish to keep the wooden stock on their Mini-14, treating the inside with some type of wood finish so that it is waterproof may help accuracy since it will help prevent swelling of the wood when exposed to moisture.

Another solution to this problem is to be sure that the forward handguard fits tightly against the stock. If there is play between the two, the accuracy will generally be poor. Use of tape or other shim material will improve this (just don't overdo the tightening, or accuracy will deteriorate). A new fiberglass handguard directly from Sturm, Ruger would also be worth trying, as would a handguard from Choate or Ram-Line.

Lack of accuracy with a standard Mini-14 can also sometimes be traced to the rifle's rear sight which may have a bit of wobble. To cure this problem, glue a small shim under the sight assembly after it has been zeroed. (With the Ranch Rifle, take care not to hit the rear sight against anything, as this can shift the rifle's zero.) For those interested in extreme accuracy, it is also possible to cut extra notches into the sighting knobs on the standard rifle (or have a gunsmith do such work). This will reduce the bullet placement by one half, i.e., down to 0.75 inch for each click when the rifle is being zeroed.

A scope will improve things for most shooters. If you're planning on using a scope, purchasing the Ranch Rifle version of the Mini-14 up front allows you to avoid purchasing a scope mount adapter. Two of the best aftermarket mounts are the Pachmayr and B-Square; these work well on the standard Mini-14 (181-series or later).

Some scope mounts are poor if you're concerned with accuracy. Perhaps the worst scope mount ever offered in terms of accuracy (made by a company which will remain nameless since they've since discontinued the mount and have some other fine accessories) was designed so that it is held in place by removing the rear sight and placing the mount in the sight well. This mount works well until a long string of shots is fired; when this is done, the heat from the barrel may cause the zero to walk off to one side. If you wish to use a scope, avoid such a mount. It still turns up in the used-gun market or at gun shows. See the appendix for more information on scope mounts.

The rifle's zero may also be changed slightly by adding a bayonet or flash suppressor. The rifle should be re-zeroed, if possible, after anything has been added to or removed from the barrel.

Use of 360-degree sling swivels which attach to the barrel may also change the point of impact, especially if a hasty sling hold is used. Such swivels are better left off the barrel unless their use is really justified.

For the utmost in accuracy, and often an increase in bullet velocity and a decrease in muzzle blast, a longer heavy barrel can be purchased to replace the factory barrel. These barrels must be placed on the rifle by a gunsmith and carefull headspaced. SGW carries two models of barrels; both are 20 inches long and made of 4140 chrome molybdenum steel. One is a "heavy barrel" which requires a lot of special gunsmith fitting to get into place and the othcr is a "standard" harrel. Both currently retail for $135. Mini-14 owners considering such a modification should remember that the trade-off for the added accuracy with a heavy barrel is added weight. Mounting cither barrel on a Mini-14 is a job for a gunsmith.

Accuracy Rifle Systems also offers stainless steel or 4140 chromium molybdenum steel barrels which they will fit to the owner's Mini-14. These barrels are a lot heavier and wider than the standard Mini-14 barrel; Accuracy Systems therefore alters the gas system and other parts slightly so that the rifle will function perfectly with the new barrel. Barrels are available in 1-in-12 and 1-in-14 twists which are suitable only for 55 grain or smaller bullets, 1-in-19 twist which is most ideal for a wide range of bullets, and 1-in-7 which is not too ideal unless you use the new NATO ammunition. The .223-6mm wildcat chambering is also available with a 1-in-10 twist. A Mini-14 rebarreled by Accuracy Rifle Systems and firing good ammunition is capable of sub-inch groups at 100 yards; definitely good enough for police sniper work or long-range varminting! Accuracy Rifle Systems also does drilling and tapping for scope mounts, headspacing, trigger work, etc.

EMERGENCY REPAIR

Like other mechanical things, Ruger firearms tend to wear out faster in some areas than in others. A spare parts kit can greatly extend a rifle's useful life, provided there isn't a catastrophic accident or outlandish abuse. A well-chosen spare parts kit can make one rifle last longer than two rifles without such a kit.

Probably the most essential parts are the extractor and its spring, the hammer spring, and one or more firing pins. A more extended kit would also include some smaller parts as well as the trigger spring, recoil spring, and possibly a secondary sear, trigger, bolt and/or hammer.

One catch to buying such a kit is that Sturm, Ruger & Company currently has a policy of not selling spare firing pins or bolts to the public.

The reason Ruger doesn't sell these parts is that they

need to be carefully fitted for safety. The solution is quite simple: the owner of the rifle removes the firing pin and sends the firearm to Ruger via United Parcel Service along with a note asking for the cost of a replacement part (a phone call is even quicker). The owner then pays for the work and the rifle is returned with a new firing pin. The Mini-14 owner then has a spare pin, carefully fitted to his rifle. Other parts, except for the bolt, which would have to be obtained in the same manner as the firing pin, are readily available from Ruger's Produce Service Department for a nominal price. Prices are usually listed in new owner's manuals which should come with the rifle. If you don't have a manual with your rifle, contact Ruger for a free one.

Currently, it is also sometimes possible to purchase the firing pin from companies carrying Mini-14 parts. A good source of Mini-14 parts is Numrich Arms Corporation. Another possible source for a firing pin is J & L Enterprises. If mail-order firing pins are purchased, it is wise to have them checked in the rifle they may be used in by a gunsmith to be sure they will function properly.

Even if you don't plan on doing any repair work yourself, the firing pin and many other parts are easily replaced by a gunsmith; having spare parts can speed up repair time, since the gunsmith won't have to send off for the parts or—in the case of the firing pin—send your rifle back to Ruger to get the work done.

When ordering spare parts from Sturm, Ruger or other companies, be sure to include your rifle's model and serial number; there are slight variations in parts from one model to another or even within one model grouping. Having a part designed for the rifle it is made for can save a lot of fitting problems.

COMPLETE DISASSEMBLY

It is seldom necessary to disassemble the Mini-14 beyond the field-stripping stage. The rifle should not be disassembled unless it is absolutely necessary; as the old saying goes, "If it's not broke, don't fix it." Every time a firearm is disassembled, it will take some time for parts to regain their fit and some may tend to shake loose with firing after being disassembled. Don't disassemble a rifle just to see if you can do it; it will probably downgrade the firearm's performance. For the same reason, skip any steps not necessary to get to the area being repaired or worked on.

Ideally, these disassembly steps would *not* be carried out by anyone other than a competent gunsmith. However, in a survival or combat situation where not having an operating firearm is a life-or-death situation, trying to carry out such work might be justified if doing nothing would be life-threatening. The costs will have to be weighed in such a case.

To disassemble the Mini-14 (see exploded diagrams) or the M14, first carry out steps one through seven in the field-stripping section. This done, carry out the following steps:

8) Use an Allen wrench to remove the four screws (2-9) which hold the gas block/front sling swivel together. It may be necessary to grind away part of the screws in order to remove them since on many Mini-14s the screws are staked or the threads flattened to keep them from shaking loose. The gas port bushing (2-6) and gas tube (2-7) will come loose when the screws are removed. When replacing the screws, use Loctite or stake the screws so that they won't shake loose during firing.

9) With the receiver top up, slide the bolt lock cover plate (3-21) down and out. This step is omitted with 180-series rifles, which don't have this plate.

10) On the top left receiver rail, depress the bolt lock plunger (3-8) and take out the bolt stop (3-18) which is also the ejector on the Ranch Rifle. Removal of the bolt stop will release the plunger (3-8) which can be released gradually and removed along with its spring (3-11) through the top of the receiver.

11) Use a drift punch or other small tool to remove the magazine catch retaining pin (these are only on the standard model Mini-14s) and remove the magazine catch from

the front of the magazine well (do this only if necessary). The rear magazine release assembly (5-11) on the front of the trigger group can also be removed with the drift punch. This should be done only if absolutely necessary, as the magazine release spring (5-10) is under extreme pressure which makes reassembly very difficult.

12) Use a screwdriver or other small tool to depress the extractor plunger (4-5) and remove the extractor (4-6). Be careful to maintain control of the spring (4-4) as it is released so that it doesn't propel itself or the plunger out.

13) Removal of the extractor will free the firing pin (4-7) so that it can be taken out the rear of the bolt (4-1).

14) Close the trigger guard (5-16) and place a drift punch or a small nail into the hole in the base of the hammer strut (5-3). Hold the hammer (5-1) and move the safety into the forward "fire" position. Pull the trigger (5-13) until the hammer is released. The hammer spring (5-2) and its strut can now be moved to the right and removed. Be careful to contain the fully compressed hammer spring as it is released.

15) Use a drift punch to remove the hammer pivot pin (5-6) and move the hammer to the right and remove it.

16) Move the safety to the "safe" position and pull the trigger guard down and to the rear to remove it.

17) Use the drift punch to remove the safety spring retaining pin (5-5) and move the spring (5-14) to the rear and unhook it from the safety. Take this spring out by moving it to the rear.

18) Use the drift punch to remove the trigger pivot pin (5-15) while restraining the trigger (5-13) and secondary sear (5-4). This will release the secondary sear, trigger, and trigger spring (5-12) for removal.

19) Use a drift punch or roll-pin punch to separate the trigger and secondary sear if necessary. Be sure to restrain the secondary sear spring (5-8) during this operation.

20) Remove the safety (5-17) by moving it upward and forward from the trigger housing (5-9).

21) The front sight of standard models is held in place by the rear sight windage pin (3-19), which is a roll pin,

and usually epoxied on as well. To remove the front sight, drift out the roll pin (2-4) and use a leather or plastic mallet to tap the front sight (2-5) off the barrel. On some Mini-14s, it may be necessary to use a punch to drive the sight off. In such a case, the sight will either have to be replaced or carefully filed and smoothed off and re-finished. Take care not to scar the muzzle during this operation.

22-A) Except for the Ranch Rifle, the rear peep sight can be removed by depressing the elevation plunger (3-10) and unscrewing the site adjustment (3-5) until the peep sight (3-2) is free. The windage knob (3-1) can be removed by drifting out the pin (3-19) that holds it in place at the right side of the rear sight. This is also the operation for removing the rear sight assembly.

22-B) On the Ranch Rifle, the rear sight can be removed by taking out the hex nut used for windage adjustments. The peep sight can be removed by taking out the two adjustment screws on its face.

23) The barrel (2-3) screws into the receiver (3-16). Barrel removal should be attempted only if there are a barrel vise and headspacing gauges available to check the barrel when it is replaced. Great care must also be taken not to damage the barrel or receiver during this procedure.

24) The stock reinforcement insert (1-4) (which the trigger assembly locks into) can be removed by the screws (1-6) on either side of the stock (1-3), squeezing the reinforcement insert together slightly, and lifting it out. This will free the forearm liner (1-2) which can then be lifted up and forward to take it out of the stock.

25) The butt plate can be removed by unscrewing the screw at its top.

REASSEMBLY

Reassembly is basically the reversal of the above procedures. Before disassembly, it's wise to study the assembled rifle so that you can more easily reassemble it rather than end up with a massive jigsaw puzzle after disassembly. The owner's manual is also very useful—especially the exploded diagram—in showing the parts relationship in whatever version of the rifle you are working on.

When putting the trigger assembly together, be sure that you place the safety spring (5-14) so that its front extension goes to the right side of the rear arm of the magazine release spring (5-10).

Small parts should be kept in some type of container during disassembly so that they aren't lost (plastic ice cube trays work nicely for this).

During reassembly, use minimum force to prevent damaging parts and to avoid incorrect part placement. If parts don't seem to fit correctly, something is wrong with how you're reassembling them.

TROUBLESHOOTING

While sportsmen can put up with occasional firearm failures, it is more enjoyable when a sporter rifle functions without failure. In combat, weapon failure can prove fatal to its owner. If your rifle is to serve as a survival weapon or be used in extended combat, you may need to replace parts when they show signs of excessive wear rather than wait for them to break. A spare parts kit like that mentioned previously would be wise to have. You should also have a number of spare magazines and cleaning gear.

One way to ensure reliability is to be sure that the ammunition and magazines used in a weapon are good. A large percentage of weapon malfunctions can be directly traced to poor ammunition and magazines.

As with any other rifle, a diet of "hot" loads in the Mini-14 will greatly shorten its life. Since the Mini-14 can function with a wide range of ammunition, reloaders should go for lighter loads that avoid creating excessive pressures in it; doing so will greatly increase the life of the rifle. Reloaders should be careful to use cannelured bullets and carefully crimp the brass so that the bullets can't be shoved back into the cartridge during chambering, creating dangerous pressure levels.

The Mini-14 should be broken in just like other firearms. Like most machinery, firearms come from the manufacturer with some rough edges, etc. These quickly wear down as the weapon is used so that after several hundred rounds go through a firearm, it will often custom-fit its parts and function very reliably from then on. Your first task after becoming familiar with your Mini-14 is to run a couple of hundred rounds through it.

Keep your rifle clean and have any problems checked out by a competent gunsmith. While the Mini-14 can be filled with grime and still work, all weapons will fail eventually, given enough dirt in their action and chambers, and the Ruger rifles are no exception. Grit will also cause a rifle to wear out very quickly. A clean weapon lasts longer and is less apt to fail than an identical—but dirty—firearm.

At the other extreme of things to avoid is overlubricating. Overoiling your weapon will actually attract dirt to its mechanism and may even deactivate a chambered round. Oil or grease in the barrel may cause the barrel to rupture or create a "goose egg" in the barrel when the gun is fired. Don't overdo your cleaning and be sure the bore is clear when you're finished.

Don't try any do-it-yourself modifications or gunsmith work unless you really know what you're doing. A gunsmith once confided to me that most of his business came from "kitchen-table gunsmiths." Don't try to fix even a simple problem unless you know exactly what you're doing. The same applies to accessories: don't buy any unless you really need them.

If a Mini-14 fails to fire, there are some quick steps that you should go through to be sure that some simple thing hasn't caused the failure:

1) Tap the magazine to be sure it's seated.

2) Pull back on the charging lever; check that a case is ejected and be sure a shell isn't jammed in the weapon.

3) If the chamber is clear, release the charging handle

to chamber a new round. Do not "ride" the bolt forward. Pulling back slightly on the bolt will enable you to check to see if a round has been chambered. Be sure the bolt is again fully seated after you've determined this.

4) Check the safety to be sure the rifle is ready to fire.

5) Try to fire again.

6) If the rifle fails to fire, go over steps one through five one more time.

7) If your rifle still fails to function, remove the magazine, cycle the weapon to be sure it's empty and check out the inside of the ejection port while you pull back the bolt. This may reveal a problem in the form of dirt or a broken part.

8) If you haven't found the fault, change magazines, cycle the action, and try firing again.

Despite these steps and the care you take in keeping your weapon clean and well maintained, your rifle may fail sometime. If you're just plinking or hunting, take it to a gunsmith to get it repaired. If you're using the rifle in a combat or survival situation, knowing how to get it functioning again may mean the difference between life and death. So read and study the procedures below so you know what to do if you should have to try to get your rifle into firing condition on your own. Do not carry out any of these procedures unless failing to do so would endanger your life.

These procedures are dangerous. If your life isn't on the line, don't attempt the actual measures with live ammunition. The best way to get a firearm fixed is to take it to a gunsmith!

It should also be noted that there are slight differences in some parts and among the various series and models of the Ruger rifles. Some of these steps may not apply to the weapon you're having problems with.

MINI-14 TROUBLESHOOTING PROCEDURES

PROBLEM	CHECK FOR	PROCEDURE
1) Bolt does not hold open after last round.	Fouled or broken bolt latch.	Clean or replace.
	Bad magazine.	Discard magazine.
2) Bolt is hung up in receiver.	Round jammed between bolt and charging handle.	DANGER: *Stay clear of the muzzle.* Remove the magazine; hold the charging handle back and slam the butt of the firearm against the ground. CAUTION: When round is freed, the bolt remains under tension.
3) Bolt won't unlock.	Dirty or burred bolt.	Clean or replace.
4) Bolt won't lock.	Fouling in locking lugs.	Clean and lubricate lugs.
	Frozen extractor (in down position) and recoil spring not moving freely.	Remove and clean extractor. Remove, clean, and lubricate.

MINI-14 TROUBLESHOOTING PROCEDURES

PROBLEM	CHECK FOR	PROCEDURE
	Bolt not moving freely.	Remove, clean and lubricate.
	Gas piston misaligned.	Check alignment; replace or realign.
	Loose or damaged piston.	Tighten or replace.
5) Double feeding.	Defective magazine.	Replace.
6) Firearm won't cock; selector doesn't work properly.	Worn, broken, or missing parts.	Check parts; replace.
7) Firearm continues to fire after release of trigger.	Dirt in trigger or sear.	Clean mechanism.
	Broken sear or trigger.	Replace.
	Weak sear or trigger spring.	Replace spring.
8) Firearm won't fire.	Safety in "safe" position.	Place in "fire" position.
	Firing pin broken.	Replace.

Problem	Cause	Remedy
	Too much oil or dirt in firing-pin recess.	Wipe or clean.
	Poor ammo.	Remove and discard.
	Weak or broken hammer or hammer spring.	Replace.
	Bolt not locking.	Clean dirty parts.
9) Round won't chamber.	Dirty or corroded ammo.	Clean ammo.
	Damaged ammo.	Replace.
	Fouling in chamber.	Clean with chamber brush.
10) Rounds won't eject.	Broken ejector.	Replace.
	Frozen ejector.	Clean or lubricate.
	Bad ejector spring.	Replace.
11) Rounds won't extract.	Broken extractor or bad extractor spring.	Replace.
	Dirty or corroded ammo.	Remove (may have to be

MINI-14 TROUBLESHOOTING PROCEDURES

PROBLEM	CHECK FOR	PROCEDURE
		carefully pushed out with cleaning rod).
	Carbon or fouling in chamber or extractor lip.	Clean chamber and lip.
	Dirty or faulty recoil spring.	Clean or replace.
12) Rounds won't feed.	Dirty or corroded ammo.	Clean off ammo.
	Low-powered ammo.	Use different ammo.
	Defective magazine.	Replace magazine.
	Dirt in magazine.	Clean and lubricate magazine.
	Too many rounds in magazine.	Remove several rounds.
	Insufficient gas to cycle action fully.	Clean all gas port gas rods, etc.
	Magazine not seated.	Reseat or replace magazine.

13) Selector lever binds.	Broken magazine catch.	Repair or replace.
	Fouling or lack of lubrication.	Lubricate; if it still binds, disassemble and clean.
14) Short recoil (new rounds fail to chamber.)	Poor ammunition.	Replace.
	Fouling in gas port.	Clean gas port.
	Damaged piston.	Repair or replace.

4.

Accessories

There's seemingly no end to the gadgets and accessories made for the Mini-14. Whether you're using the rifle to fight groundhogs or enemy troops, it's a big mistake to have too much gear. A good rifle, quality ammunition, and reliable magazines are the essentials for safe and enjoyable shooting. If you have only these, you won't be doing too poorly. Bayonets, bipods, special stocks, electric scopes, etc., can all be of use in some situations but are often just so much extra weight.

Some accessories are outright junk. If you aren't being supplied by a government agency or the like, be careful what you spend your hard-earned cash on. Many snazzy accessories literally fall apart with hard use. Don't be the first to buy a piece of new gear; listen to what others have to say about something. (A few publications give the straight scoop rather than manufacturers' press releases on new equipment. One magazine that I've found to be especially objective is *American Rifleman*.) Poor equipment often quickly gains a bad reputation; look and listen before you buy.

For combat, you may wish to consider the following: your Mini-14, and four to six 20- or 30-round magazines.

And nothing else.

Consider throwing in a good pocket knife, preferably with a screwdriver blade, odds and ends of a first-aid kit, a canteen if you'll be out for long periods, maybe a rifle sling (Uncle Mike's are good buys), and maybe a long-bladed combat knife like the SI-5 Eickhart combat knife or the Bundeswehr knife (both are available from Sherwood International). A .22 pistol like the Ruger Mark II or a small backup pistol like the Jennings J-22 is only needed if you'll also be supplying yourself with meat or are in a survival situation.

All this gear needs to be carried. You'll need a belt and harness with pouches, a combat vest, or some such arrangement. Military harnesses and pouches usually aren't called for unless you're getting ready for the Battle of the Bulge. Lightweight commercial pouches and belts like those put out by Uncle Mike's make a lot more sense.

When you have your gear, it's important to try it all out. Finding that some bits of gear aren't compatible or needed should happen before you're out in the woods. Test

Whether hunting or fighting, the accessories and gear that you need should be carried in some type of belt/pouch arrangement. Some of the best belts and pouches are available from Uncle Mike's. This tough nylon gear is ideal for carrying the essentials—like a Hershey's chocolate bar. Photo courtesy of Michaels of Oregon.

Uncle Mike's miniature belt pouches are ideal for such field necessities as compasses and 5-round magazines. Photo courtesy of Michaels of Oregon.

things out ahead of time and discard some gear if it isn't working out.

Try to avoid accessories that need a hex driver or L-wrench to attach or remove from your Mini-14. If you do use such an accessory, either carry the tool or replace the special screws with standard slot-headed screws or wing nuts. A local hardware store will be able to supply you with the parts you need, or if you can't get a replacement with proper threads, you can cut a slot into the hex screws with a hacksaw for a standard screwdriver. Touch-up blue will give hardware screws or slots sawed into hex screws a dull black finish.

Don't get fragile gear. One of the laws of physics seems

to be that what can be carried will be dropped. Also consider whether or not a piece of equipment will work in dirt or heavy brush. Does it need batteries? Chances are good it won't be working when you need it.

Equipment shouldn't hamper your movement or slow you down. Loops, projections, even long magazines can all get you stuck or snagged just often enough to ruin an outing or be dangerous in combat. Duck-billed flash suppressors, slings, and heavy night-vision equipment are three examples of good equipment that can get you hung up in heavy vegetation. Many types of gear will work in some environments and not in others. Think about what can happen with the equipment you carry in the environment you'll be in.

If you're choosing equipment for combat, ask yourself if an accessory will improve your shooting ability or utility of your Mini-14 in the conditions you're expecting. If not, it probably isn't needed.

Now let's look at some specific equipment.

AT-22 RIFLE

Yes, it's probably wrong to start out the accessory section with another completely different rifle. But the Mini-14 is not called "the world's most expensive plinker" without reason. It is expensive to shoot .223 rounds. (And the same is true for the M14 and its variants or the Garand.)

The AT-22's safety, charging lever, and sight are almost identical to those of the Mini-14, so this rifle makes a very good beginner's and plinker's rifle.

The AT-22 rifle has a full-sized pistol grip that has a storage compartment inside it, large enough for survival items or extra rounds.

But, as the cliché goes, practice makes perfect. Those who become good shots do so by practicing a lot.

It is a lot cheaper to practice with .22 LR ammunition than .223 Remington, so many wise shooters either get a .22 conversion unit (listed below) or a .22 rifle that operates similarly to the Mini-14. Unfortunately, Ruger doesn't offer a .22 rifle modeled off their Mini-14 (though such a rifle may be marketed in the near future). While the 10/22 is an excellent rifle with a similar point of aim, its safety is in a completely different location and the magazine release is quite different (though Ram-Line currently offers a replacement release that extends the release so that it can be operated like the Mini-14s).

This is where the AT-22 comes in. Provided you use a Mini-14 with a pistol grip stock, the two rifles are very similar. (Many combat shooters prefer a pistol grip on their rifle since it makes it a lot easier to control and more comfortable to shoot.)

The "AT" stands for "Advanced Technology," and the

name certainly isn't a misnomer since the manufacturer makes use of aluminum and steel parts which are precision-machined on computer-controlled equipment, new plastics, and Allen-head screws and roll pins in assembling the firearm. Machining tolerances are within a five-thousandth of an inch. Even the design reflects the high-tech aspects.

The firearm was designed by L. James Sullivan, who has helped out with rifles like the AR-7, AR-10, and AR-15, along with other Armalite weapons; the Stoner 62/63 weapons; and a number of other weapons overseas. Sullivan was also one of the designers who helped Ruger when the Mini-14 was being created. (Although a lot of people think the AT-22 is a version of the AR-7 Explorer, the two weapons have little in common.)

The AT-22 rifle has a telescoping wire stock, plastic furniture, and a pistol grip with a storage compartment for ammunition or survival gear. In addition to being useful as a Mini-14-like practice rifle, it can also be used to teach young shooters. The length of pull can be downscaled by using a drill press or file to put extra adjustment notches on the stock.

The rifle is small, but has an "adult-size" pistol grip and a nice forward handguard. Recoil, since the weapon is light, is greater than might be expected with a .22, but certainly nothing to worry about even when training beginners. The increased felt recoil makes the weapon a bit more desirable for training. The big plus is that its operational layout is very similar to that of the Mini-14. The safety is located in the trigger guard and the charging lever is on the right side of the receiver. The adjustable rear peep sight's picture is very similar to that of the Mini-14. About the only major difference is that the magazine release is located just ahead of the magazine rather than to its rear. However, with its standard 20-round magazine, the AT-22 has a lot of bangs before it is necessary to reload.

The AT-22 shoots very well and is very reliable thanks to a throating cut in it to assure easy chambering of rounds. The barrel also has an excellent spring-loaded feed ramp above the chamber which pushes stray cartridges into the chamber. Both of these make for near faultless feeding. The magazine does its part as well. Its feed lips are almost directly behind the chamber so shells don't have to make any climbs. Internally, the magazine allows a slight staggering of shells so that the rims stay out of each other's way (this also allows for a straight magazine rather than a banana clip). Coupled with a positive striker action, the rifle digests any .22 LR fodder and is just as reliable as the ammunition you feed it. The AT-22 is accurate, too.

The safety of the AT-22 is located inside the trigger guard, and the charging lever is on the right side of the receiver; similarly placed to those of the Mini-14.

The rear sight of the AT-22 (which is adjustable for windage) is a peep sight so that the picture is very similar to that of the Mini-14.

The AT-22 is easily field-stripped without tools. This makes it ideal as a survival weapon in addition to being a good training rifle.

For training purposes, CCI's CB Caps can be used. This turns the AT-22 into a sort of bolt-action rifle, since the action has to be hand-cycled after each shot. For beginners, this is ideal since it makes it hard to fire a round by accident and the soft muzzle blast (which is barely audible with the CB Caps in a rifle) allows shooting without earmuffs.

The AT-22 currently retails at a little over $200. Considering the cost of .223 ammunition, if you shoot 100 rounds per training session, the AT-22 will pay for itself in ten or eleven sessions. After that, it will be saving you about $20 per session. For those who do a lot of practicing, a .22 rifle or conversion kit makes a lot of sense.

The AT-22 is a tough little rifle that you can give to a young shooter and expect to last a lifetime, length of pull growing up with the beginner. Your beginning shooter— and you—will be used to operating an action like that of the Mini-14 when the time comes to switch to one of the larger rifles. Feather Enterprises (which manufactures the AT-22) offers a Cordura carrying case, scope mounts, barrels, and spare parts for the rifle as well.

AT-22 Specifications

Length (stock extended)................... 34.75 in.
Length (stock in short position) .... 26 in
Barrel length............................... 17 in.
Magazine (standard) 20-round
Weight (approx.)..........................3.25 lbs.

BAYONETS

Brigadier General S.L.A. Marshall wrote in the May/ June 1967 issue of *Infantry* that the bayonet was *never* used for fighting on the end of a rifle in Vietnam. Rather, troops in Vietnam learned that empty rifles, entrenching tools, hunting knives, etc., were better hand-to-hand combat weapons. Modern battlefields and the high rate of firepower of modern weapons have made the chances of needing a bayonet on the end of a rifle very small indeed.

Bayonets do make good fighting knives and are relatively inexpensive as such. If you need a fighting knife, consider a bayonet. Try Sherwood International; they have a huge selection of modern, well-made bayonets.

Choate and several other companies offer bayonet mounts which allow the use of an M16 bayonet on a Mini-14. However, it is wise to save your money and be thankful that the mount is left off most Mini-14s.

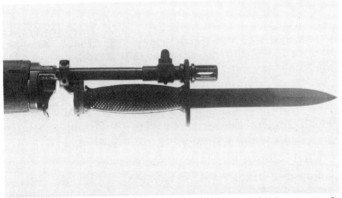

Choate offers a bayonet mount which allows an M16 bayonet to be mounted on a Mini-14. Also shown is the Choate AR-15-style flash suppressor. Photo courtesy of Choate Machine and Tool.

BIPODS

Like the bayonet, the bipod is nearly useless in combat. It looks nifty and helps display rifles at gun shows, but most bipods used out in the wilds are too short to allow you to see what you're shooting at. Unless you're using your Mini-14 for sniping or varminting, you'll usually do well to forget a bipod; for varminting or sniping, a bipod can allow a shooter to spend a lot of time shooting without moving his point of aim or getting arm cramps.

Harris bipods come in two models. One model extends from eight to 13 inches and is ideal for prone shooting, while the other (shown here with the Ranch Rifle) extends from 13 to 23 inches which allows shooting from a seated position. Photo courtesy of Harris Engineering, Inc.

Currently there are several types of "clothespin" bipods which clip onto the barrel of a Mini-14. The military bipod designed for the AR-15 will work if you glue some rubber strips inside it to take up the slack between the larger dimensions of the AR-15 barrel. Many of these bipods are rust-prone, however, and there are better ones available.

Probably the best of the clothespin types is the Ram-Line nylon bipod which works the same way as the military

Harris bipods attach directly to the stock of the rifle so that there is absolutely no barrel flex; the zero stays the same if the bipod is in use or if you're standing and firing with the bipod still attached. Photo courtesy of Harris Engineering, Inc.

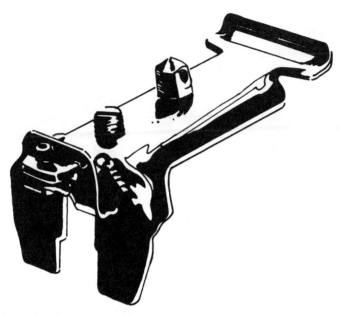

A special adapter is needed to mount the Harris bipod on the Mini-14 rifles.

Among the best adjustable bipods are those made by Harris. Straightforward to use, Ultralight Bipods only look complex. Photo courtesy of Harris Engineering, Inc.

model but will fit almost any diameter barrel and is less apt to mar the finish. Rum Line bipods retail at around $15 each and have become very popular.

Among the best adjustable bipods are those made by Harris. Their Ultralight bipods look complex but are pretty straightforward to use. A special adapter is needed to use them with the Mini-14 rifle (this costs about $15). The nice thing about Harris bipods is that they attach to the stock of the rifle, so that there is absolutely no barrel flex; zero stays the same if the bipod is in use or if you're standing and firing with the bipod still attached. Two models are available. One extends from eight to 13 inches and is ideal for prone shooting while the other extends from 13 to 23 inches which allows you to fire from a seated position (a plus in an area with tall weeds and grass). Either version costs $40.

Another good bipod is the "Wooley Bugar" currently marketed by Choate Machine and Tool for $48. This unit is all steel and attaches to the barrel. Ideally, this unit should be placed close to the stock so that the weight of the bipod won't cause the point of impact to change.

BRASS CATCHERS

E & L Manufacturing makes a good rigid brass catcher for the Mini-14. The E & L Rigid Brass Catcher works well and can save you a lot of time and money if you reload (just don't try to use a brass catcher in combat). It's great for practice since it also helps you to avoid developing the terrible habit of trying to watch where brass goes (a trait that's gotten some policemen killed in combat).

There are two models of the E & L catcher; one is for the standard Mini-14 and the other for the Ranch Rifle.

CALIBER CONVERSION

A .22 LR conversion unit is available for all Mini-14s except the 180-series and is easily installed. With its 30-round magazine and low recoil, the .22 conversion is perfect for training or plinking. Like the AT-22, this conversion can be used with .22 LR ammunition or CCI's Long CB Caps. The conversion unit can be ordered directly from Jonathan Arthur Ciener, Inc., for about $99.

Harry Owen's less expensive conversion units offer a trade-off for the lower price in some awkwardness; the units must be chambered by hand and require a bit of work to reload. The Harry Owen conversion units are made of brass or steel and look like an empty cartridge. A smaller cartridge is placed inside the adapter and a striker is placed behind it. When the adapter is chambered, the Mini-14's firing pin hits the striker which fires the cartridge. The unit is then carefully extracted and a small rod used to push out the striker and spent casing.

The Harry Owen adapters come in several versions. The .22 LR version can fire .22 LR (standard or high velocity), .22 Long, .22 Short, .22 shot cartridges, .22 CB Long, etc. Another conversion unit allows the use of .22 Magnum cartridges in the Mini-14. Both .22 bullets are close enough in size to the .223 Remington bullet to allow good accuracy. These adapters cost around $19 each for the brass model or $27 for the steel version.

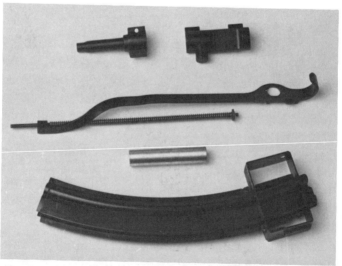

The Jonathan Arthur Ciener .22 LR conversion kit for the Mini-14 works well and is easy to install. It fits all Mini-14s except the 180 series of rifles. Photo courtesy of Jonathan Arthur Ciener, Inc.

The Jonathan Arthur Ciener .22 LR adapter kit is shown here as it looks installed in a stainless steel Mini-14. Photo courtesy of Jonathan Arthur Ciener, Inc.

Another Harry Owen adapter is for air rifle pellets. This requires the use of a rifle primer which is placed at the end of the unit. A .22 air rifle pellet is then placed in the adapter; when the cartridge is chambered and fired, the pellet is propelled out of the Mini-14 with no little force but without much noise. This unit, along with a depriming rod, is available for $24.

For the M14, similar adapters are also available from Harry Owen. Because of the difference in barrel diameter, the .308 adapter has a small barrel built into it to give the bullets stabilizing spin and velocity. Like the .223 adapter, the .308 version allows the use of a wide range of .22 rimfire cartridges. Adapters are also available for use with .30 caliber cartridges like the .30 Carbine. The .22 adapters cost $35 each; those for .30 caliber cartridges, which don't need the rifled section, cost $19 for brass models or $27 for steel.

(For those who reload ammunition, it is also possible to create "squib" loads which have the low energy/velocity levels needed for quiet practice, hunting small game, etc. Besides being a lot less expensive to shoot, squib loads can be cycled through the magazine of the rifle without the shooter having to chamber each one by hand as is the case with the Harry Owen adapters.)

In addition to adapters, conversion barrels are available to convert the Mini-14 to the 6mm .223 Wildcat. This cartridge consists of standard .223 brass reformed so the neck holds a 70- to 100-grain 6mm bullet. The cartridge doesn't have much edge ballistically over the .223 but may be legal to use for hunting deer in some states. (For hunting such animals, shot placement must be precise and at rather close ranges.) Standard .223 magazines will work with this cartridge. Currently, such work is being done by Accuracy Rifle Systems. Because of the expense of rebarreling a rifle, it might be wiser to purchase a Rancher Rifle in 7.62 × 39mm or an M14 variant in .308 Winchester for hunting medium-sized game and a wide range of game, respectively. Cartridges can also be down-loaded for use with smaller animals and hand cycled through the M14's .308 action.

A similar barrel conversion is offered by Teton Arms for the .17 Remington round. This cartridge uses 25-grain bullets (with a muzzle velocity of 3,000 to 4,000 fps!). Based on a necked-down .223 cartridge but available commercially, this cartridge is suited only for small varmint shooting, so anyone considering such a conversion should be sure they don't mind limiting themselves.

CAMOUFLAGE

If you need to camouflage clothing and gear, the "designer black" or "stick out stainless" of the Mini-14 rifles may be less than ideal. Many shooters have spooked an animal or been discovered by an enemy because their uncamouflaged gun caught an eye.

Cloth covers for the Mini-14 are available from Military Surplus Supply for $19 a set. The covers use Velcro fasteners and are quick to attach and remove, but they only cover the stock so you'll need to use camo tape or rags to cover the barrel.

A better route, if you can follow it, is just to paint your weapon. Spray paint works well. First plug up the barrel and cover moving parts so the firearm won't get gummed up. Also, be sure to use acetone to remove any oil that will cause paint not to stick to the rifle's surface. This done, first spray-paint the rifle with the dominant color. Next, after the paint has dried, cut out paper stencils, tape them to the rifle and add another color. Once that's dried, tape more stencils onto the rifle and again cover it with paint. When the third coat has dried, peel off the various sten cils and you should have a camo rifle.

It's wise to practice on some old pipe or boards so that you perfect your technique a bit before having at your expensive rifle. One quick-and-dirty method of creating stencils for the paint consists of piling leaves and foliage from the area you'll be in on the rifle between coats of paint. Although this requires painting each side of the rifle separately, it is generally easier and does give some natural-looking patterns to the camouflaged layout.

Brigade Quartermasters currently offers a set of four cans of paint (brown, olive drab, black, and tan) which are ideally suited for this purpose at $17 for the set.

Camo tape designed for hunters is also ideal if you may need to sell your weapon later on or have several seasonal changes to contend with (a green and brown gun in the snow is hardly camouflaged). Brigade Quartermasters also carries this tape and has three styles of camo tape (green, brown, and grey). The tape is available for $6 per roll (one roll will cover one gun).

CARRYING CASES

Carrying cases are good to store or transport a firearm in a car or truck. A case allows you to carry the rifle through a populated area and also protects it from small bumps and scratches.

Assault Systems makes very good Cordura nylon cases. Available in black or camo, these cases have thick padding, and the nylon shell holds up well.

If you only need a carrying case occasionally, then it makes sense to get one of the less-expensive cloth cases. The best ones are made of a heavy canvas (camo, black, or olive green) covering with a lint-free corduroy lining. Good ones are available for $28 each from Parellex or Sherwood International.

For carrying a rifle in a scabbard, whether you're on

horseback or charging across the country on a snowmobile, the nylon scabbards from Michaels of Oregon are
ideal. Cost is $45 for the Mini-14 size scabbard and $50
for the M14 size.

**Whether storing a Mini-14 in a closet or carrying it while on horseback
(above), a good scabbard like this from Michaels of Oregon is ideal
for protecting a rifle. Photo courtesy of Michaels of Oregon.**

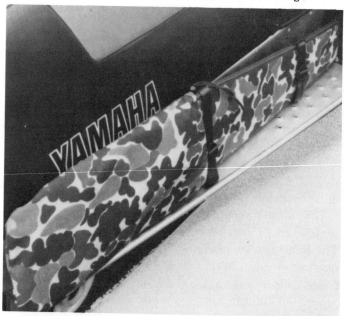

Uncle Mike's scabbards make carrying a rifle on a snowmobile...

...or on a motorcycle...

...easy, and keep from alarming those not accustomed to seeing guns being carried. Photos courtesy of Michaels of Oregon.

FLASH SUPPRESSORS AND MUZZLE BRAKES

Flash suppressors do away with much of the nighttime muzzle flash created by unburnt powder. Chances are good you'll never need such a product on your rifle unless you're really into a serious combat situation; in such a case, a flash suppressor would be a useful accessory.

Muzzle brakes are different from flash suppressors, though some units combine properties of both. The muzzle brake takes some of the energy of the gas near the muzzle and rechannels it so that it propels the barrel in a direction counter to that produced by the recoil. This jet of redirected gas can reduce muzzle climb, felt recoil, or both. The trade-off is increased muzzle flash and noise. Muzzle brakes are ideal for automatic fire and make sense on Mini-14s with automatic or burst-fire capability.

A number of companies make flash suppressors for the Mini-14. Probably the top of the line is offered by Choate, which replaces the front sight with a "dog ear" sight. Three types of these flash suppressors are available: an AR-15 "bird cage," a long "M14" style, and a suppressor which is designed for nighttime use. Choate flash suppressors do not have openings in the lower side; this gives them a bit of a muzzle-brake effect. The only down side to the Choate suppressors is that removal of the Ruger sight is hard to accomplish and the new sight has to have a hole drilled in the barrel to line it up; the work is best done by a gunsmith. Cost of any of these models is around $30 each. Finishes include both blued steel and "Nitex," which matches the finish of the stainless steel Mini-14s.

Ram-Line makes both a stainless steel and a blued finish suppressor with an M14 look to them. These slip around the front sight of the Mini-14 and don't change the sight picture much. The advantage is that these flash suppressors can easily be removed.

A competent gunsmith can cut threads into the muzzle end of a Mini-14. This allows you to use a wide range of flash suppressors and muzzle brakes designed for the AR-15.

Choate offers top-of-the-line aftermarket flash suppressors such as the M14 style (top) and the AR-15 "bird cage" suppressors. The units are available in two finishes, standard blued steel and the "Nitex" (bottom left) which matches stainless steel models. The Choate suppressors also act as effective muzzle brakes. The dog-eared sight blades give a picture similar to that of most military rifles.

Old-style duckbill flash suppressors, such as this Nil-Flash, are similar to those originally on the M16, and are being made again. The Nil-Flash is available from D.C. Brennan Firearms.

Old-style duck bill flash suppressors similar to the original M16 model are also being made again. While these don't compensate for muzzle climb and are a pain in heavy vegetation, they are extremely good at reducing muzzle flash. Two of the best are the Nil-Flash, which retails from D.C. Brennan Firearms, and the Vortex from Smith Enterprises, which retails for $35 (Smith Enterprises will thread the Mini-14 barrel and mount their Vortex flash suppressor for $50).

There are two good compensators on the market which reduce muzzle flip. One is borrowed from the USSR's new AK-74. It's made by Alpha Armament and doesn't require cutting threads on the barrel; cost is $39. In addition to pushing the barrel down and to the side to compensate for recoil, it also acts like a muzzle brake and reduces felt recoil. The trade-off is increased muzzle noise and the blowing of gas to each side of the muzzle, which can be disconcerting to people around you and can raise a cloud of dust if you're close to the ground.

Another excellent compensator is the DTA Mil/Brake (formerly called the Muzzle Mizer) from Fabian Brothers Sporting Goods for $25. The Mil/Brake is available in two threadings. One is for weapons threaded for the AR-15 flash suppressor (which would be ideal for the Mini-14) and the other for .308-caliber weapons like the HK-91 and M14/M1A. Either version creates less noise and flash than the AK74-style brake. The units reduce felt recoil somewhat as well as prevent muzzle climb.

LASERS

A laser creates a beam of light that disperses very little and is highly intense. When a laser is mounted on a firearm, it is possible to pinpoint the bullet's potential impact point—within several inches since the light goes in a straight line while the bullet travels a ballistic arc. It's easy to imagine how quickly a target can be found with a laser. Too, shouldering a weapon is no longer essential. In fact, a more rigid hold and steadier aim are created with laser-aiming systems by holding the weapon in the assault carry. If any aiming system had the potential to change tactics, the laser is it. And since firing with a laser from the hip is more accurate than from the shoulder, it encourages a "heads up" view of what is going on around you. So why isn't everyone running out to get one? Price. They're expensive, fragile, and need massive battery systems that quickly run down. Laser-aiming systems aren't for everyone.

(Some laser systems are a lot better than others. Before you shell out your cash, try the laser out. And be sure it *cannot* be seen from the enemy end of things. If it can, you'll be creating a bright red aiming point for your foe.)

At least one company, Laser Products, currently markets a Mini-14 with a built-in laser system. They use a standard Mini-14, place the laser batteries in the stock, and mount the laser tube below the rifle's barrel. This makes a weapon that is easy to handle and does away with projections which can be bumped or get hung up in brush. The rifle and laser unit weigh ten pounds and give 40 to 60 minutes of continuous operation on fully charged rechargeable batteries.

Sources to check for laser systems are Laser Arms Corp., Laser Products, Hydra Systems, and Executive Protection Products. The "low range" versions cost around $500.

MAGAZINES

One of the most important parts of the Mini-14 (and all other rifles) is the magazine. If you have a poor magazine, the rifle is apt to fail. The best magazines to have for the Mini-14 are made by Sturm, Ruger. They fit well and function perfectly.

Aftermarket magazines do, however, sometimes offer a savings in initial price and are available in configurations not available from Ruger. When you purchase any magazines, especially aftermarket magazines, test them out in the rifle to be sure they function flawlessly.

The M14 magazine is well designed and usually works

well in the variants of this rifle. These are currently available from Sherwood International for $17 each. Tobias Guns also offers a plastic 30 round magazine which will work in the M14 and its variants.

For 20-, 30-, or 40-round metal magazines for the Mini-14, the best sources are Parellex and Sherwood International. Costs are in the neighborhood of $10 for the 20-round, $13 for the 30-round, and $25 for the 40-round magazine from either company. Sherwood International also offers nickel-coated magazines for $3 to $4 more a piece.

Because the Mini-14 magazine is similar in size to the AR-15/M16 magazine, a few enterprising souls have altered M16 magazines to fit into the Ruger rifle. This is a route best avoided if the rifle is going to be used in a survival or combat situation.

Ram-Line currently markets a plastic "Combo-Mag" which can be used in the Mini-14, AR-15, AR-180, or other rifles. If you own several different rifles, these are worth considering. The magazines come in two styles (clear or smoked plastic) and cost around $14 each. The only problem that some shooters may find is that these magazines may fail to hold the bolt open with the last shot.

Regardless of the brand, new magazines often have sharp edges on the lip that the rounds have to travel over. Use a small file or sharp steel blade to carefully round off this edge. This will often increase the reliability of a magazine/rifle immeasurably and is worth the little extra effort involved.

Numerous ways have been developed to couple magazines together. One way not to connect magazines is to tape them together so that one magazine's lips are up when the other's are down. If the shooter ever has to fire from the prone position or bumps the magazine against something, he is apt to discover it has become full of dirt or the lips are bent. A better solution is the connector sold by Choate. This consists of two metal plates separated by a metal spacer. The plates are bolted together on either side of two magazines so that one sits alongside

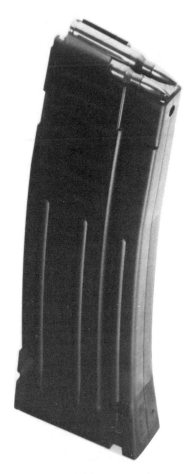

Ram-Line markets the "Combo Mag," available in clear or smoked plastic, which may be used in the Mini-14, AR-15, AR-180 and other rifles. Photo courtesy of Ram-Line.

the other. This makes it easy to change magazines and makes the magazine not in use less apt to become damaged or full of dirt.

The Redi-Mag from JFS consists of a mechanism that attaches to the rifle itself and allows the shooter to place a standard magazine in it. When the magazine is released from the rifle, the spare comes loose as well. This allows the shooter to grasp both magazines at once and quickly place the new magazine in the rifle's well. The Redi-Mag also allows the use of standard magazines without adding anything to them. Because of this, the magazines can be carried without special pouches.

Government surplus stripper clips are of great use to recharge a magazine. These can be purchased from Sierra Supply and allow a shooter to carry ten rounds of .223 on each clip. By bending the GI charging tool slightly, the clips can be used to feed rounds into most Ruger magazines. Better yet, purchase Choate's stripper clip guide for $10. It allows you to quickly recharge a magazine with stripper clips. Don't try to substitute clips for loaded magazines in a combat situation; they are a little too slow when the pressure is on. With the M14 variants, military surplus stripper clips and charging tools will generally work perfectly. The extended .223 and .308 magazines can usually be carried in military surplus pouches designed for use with either the M16 (for the Mini-14) or the M14. These are generally readily available from companies like Brigade Quartermaster.

For combat, many find combat vests even better than magazine pouches. These vests have pouches for magazines and other gear and can be donned at a moment's notice. One of the best buys in vests is the Combat Support Vest from Newman's GI Supply. It's available in a rifle and submachine gun model (according to the size of the magazines used) and costs $76.

MARLIN MODEL 45 AND MODEL 9 "CAMP CARBINES"

Although these two Marlin rifles bear little internal resemblance to the Mini-14 or M14, like the AT-22, they operate and handle similarly to the Ruger rifles. This makes them ideal for switching from one rifle to another with a minimum of problems.

The Marlin Model 45 is chambered for the .45 ACP pistol cartridge and the Model 9 is chambered for the 9mm Luger. Both have a charging lever on the right side and a Garand-style safety similar to that of the Mini-14. The only major difference is that the magazine release is located on the left side of the Marlin rifles. This could probably be modified to the Ruger style by a good gunsmith, though it is doubtful that such work would be needed by most shooters.

The sight picture of the Marlin rifles is slightly different from that of the Mini-14. The rear sight has a "V" blade and the front is a hooded ramp with a brass bead. These can easily be changed, however; the hood can be removed by the owner and any competent gunsmith can easily change the rear sight to an aperture style. The steel receiver is drilled and tapped for a scope mount.

The Model 45 and Model 9 both fire from a closed bolt with the standard blowback design. The Model 45 comes with a 7-round magazine, and 12- and 20-round magazines are available for the Model 9.

Either Marlin rifle is suitable for smaller game for which the Mini-14 is much too powerful. For those needing a carbine for self-defense where rifle bullets are too powerful, the Marlin rifles would be ideal if loaded with expanding bullets. The longer barrel of these rifles gives a lot more energy to pistol bullets and also reduces muzzle blast. With the 9mm, a 22 percent increase in muzzle velocity occurs with many brands of ammunition; similar results can be expected in .45.

Both models of the Marlin rifle are reliable, but like many other firearms, they are a little prone to functioning problems when they become heavily fouled. Therefore, care must be taken to keep the rifles clean and lubricated according to the manufacturer's recommendations.

For those wanting a family of weapons with identical safeties, point of aim, etc., the Marlin rifles are ideal for adding to the Mini-14 family.

Marlin Model 45 and Model 9 Specifications

Barrel length . . . . 16.5 in.
Calibers . . . . 9mm Luger and .45 ACP
Length (approx.). . . . . 35.5 in.
Weight unloaded (approx.) . . . . .6.5 lbs.

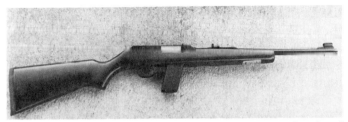

The Marlin Model 9 (chambered in 9mm Luger, shown above) and the Marlin Model 45 (in .45 ACP) are very similar in manual operation to the Mini-14; each of the rifles has a charging lever on the right side of the receiver and a Garand-style safety. Because of their chamberings, the Marlin rifles are better suited for some chores than is the Mini-14.

NIGHT SIGHTS

Glow-in-the-dark sights can help you find a target at night. One device of use in nighttime shooting is the Nightsighter available from Light Enterprises for $18. This accessory uses a small light-emitting diode and two inexpensive digital watch batteries to create a tiny spot of light which can be lined up with the front sight. A set of batteries will give continuous light for several months. The unit clamps behind the rear sight so that normal use of the sights can be made during the day.

You'll need to practice a lot at getting the weapon lined up properly to use this sight or one of the dot sights listed below. Practice is easy: close your eyes, shoulder the weapon, then open your eyes to check your "zero."

NIGHT-VISION SCOPES

If you thought lasers were expensive, check into night-vision equipment! The current scopes are also heavy. A night-vision scope on a rifle turns it into a nice imitation of an anchor.

Two types of night-vision scopes are available: active and passive. Active systems use an infrared spotlight to light up the view for their scope; they can "see" in darker conditions but are easy to spot by someone else with a similar scope. Active units make nice targets when your enemy also has one.

Passive units are glorified television cameras that boost available light and show what's out there on a miniature greenish screen. They work on moonlight, starlight, city glow, etc. Passive units can't be spotted as easily as active units.

There are two generations of passive night-vision devices, with a third on the way. First-generation scopes work well provided you don't have to view an area that is partially lit. A bright light in a dark area creates streaking and blooming which can fog up areas of the screen for several seconds. This handicap goes with a lower price tag, though, so many buyers may want first-generation equipment.

The second-generation scope is smaller and can deal with lights, flares, etc. It can also be left mounted on a firearm and, with a special filter, can work day or night.

A good passive scope costs from $2,000 to $15,000 while more bulky active scopes will range from $500 to $1,000. Both need to have batteries recharged or replaced from time to time and are easily damaged. Little wonder they aren't too prevalent on the battlefield.

Major companies making night-vision equipment for combat weapons include Excalibur Enterprises, Litton (Electron Tube Division), and Standard Equipment Co.

REAR SIGHTS

For those not happy with the standard Mini-14 rear sight, there are several options available. Ram-Line and Feather Enterprises both offer hooded plastic sights, and Ram-Line also has an open "buckhorn" style rear aperture. (The peep sight is faster and better suited for combat; nevertheless, many hunters who are accustomed to "V" sights may prefer the buckhorn style.)

Williams also offers the "FP" series of micrometer rear sights for varminting or target shooting. Some gunsmithing is necessary to fit these sights to the rifle.

Millett Sights offers a replacement sight which uses the standard Mini-14 mount. The Millett sight allows windage and drop adjustments to be made with a small screwdriver which is considerably quicker than the standard bullet point system. However, because the aperture is exposed and easily damaged, the Millett sight is too fragile for hunting or combat. The sight costs $46.

SCOPES AND MOUNTS

Scopes are getting better and tougher, so much so that more and more are being found on combat weapons, with a few countries all but abandoning metal sights in favor of optical systems.

Just as important as the scope is its mounting system. Always check to be sure the mount has no play and can be easily removed. Because scopes can fail, it is wise to keep the iron sights on your Mini-14 zeroed in case you need to fall back on them.

Probably the best bet if you're going to use a scope on the Mini-14 is to purchase the Rancher Rifle. It is made for scoped use and can save you the trouble and expense of purchasing an aftermarket mount.

If you wish to scope a standard Mini-14, B-Square makes an excellent mount which requires no gunsmith work since it replaces the receiver plate over the hold-open lever (and therefore won't work on 180-series Mini-14s) and comes with its own scope rings.

With the Ranch Rifle, getting a cheek weld is no problem since the scope is mounted low on the rifle. With B-Square and other mounts, the scope may ride a little high. One solution to this is the Cheekpiece from Cherokee Gun Accessories. Though it has a $42 price tag, the urethane attachment works well and is quickly detachable.

Range-finding scopes and other variable scopes are relatively fragile and, with the flat shooting .223, of dubious value. With the .308 M14 variants, such scopes might make sense. Unless you're in a situation in which there is little chance of damaging a scope, it is usually wise to avoid buying a range-finding scope or get one of the higher grade (read "expensive") scopes. Rubber armor on a scope can help to protect your investment. The fixed scope is tougher, and most of your money goes toward optics rather than gear work. The 4X is the most versatile, though a higher power might be needed for sniping or long-range varminting.

Probably the best buys these days are the Tasco scopes, with my favorite being the brushed-finish 4 × 40mm DF 4 × 40 WA. Bausch & Lomb, Beeman (whose lenses are made by the Nikon camera company), Burris, Bushnell, Leupold, Redfield, Shepherd, Swarovski Optik, Simmons, Weatherby, and Williams are also pretty good bets. Avoid unknown bargain scopes; they are not always reliable and seldom a bargain.

When possible, get scopes with the new rubber armor coat and avoid shiny black finishes if you need to keep a low profile. Tasco and a number of others have a brushed black finish that makes a lot of sense if you can't get the rubber armor. If you have a stainless rifle, most companies offer "silver" scopes for the style-conscious.

Most scopes are advertised with two numbers: for example, 4 × 40mm. The first number is the power of the scope; the second, the size of the field of view. A wider field of view makes it possible to locate your target more easily. While this may not be a consideration for target shooters, for many others a wider field of view is a good idea.

Occasionally one sees a mount for the Mini-14 for a pistol scope mounted on the rifle's barrel. These do allow a wide field of view and might have some merit in combat. However, the scope is out front where it can be damaged, and excessive heat from firing long strings of shots can throw off accuracy. Too, since pistol scopes have long eye relief, the trade-off is a narrow field of view. Without a lot of practice, pistol scopes are often actually slower to use than iron sights.

Small "combat" scopes should also be considered for some applications since they are less apt to get hung up in brush and are lighter in weight. Probably the best of these are the SS-1 and SS-2 from Beeman. The SS-1 costs

$120 and the SS-2 $189.

Dot scopes place a dot in the field of view rather than cross hairs. Many shooters find them quicker to use. The catch is that they can also block some of the target at extreme ranges. But there are some pluses, especially with scopes that are only one power; these allow the shooter to use both eyes when aiming. This really speeds things up and allows the shooter a full field of view, important in many hunting and combat situation.

Another style of dot scope is the occluded eye scope. This scope creates a dot without any view of the target. That view is provided by the shooter's other eye. This scope is confusing to use at first, since most shooters close one eye when aiming, but once the occluded eye system is gotten used to, the system is very quick and, like the one-power dot scope, gives a wide field of view. Unlike the one-power scope, the occluded eye system can't be used by all shooters; some people have vision problems that make the dot wander about the target somewhat. Likewise, those with good vision in only one eye can't use the occluded system.

The best available-light occluded eye scopes are the Armson O.E.G. (Occluded Eye Gunsight), which costs $220, and the Singlepoint, which costs $125. Despite the extra expense, I prefer the glow-red dot of the O.E.G. since it is smaller and easier to find than the white dot of the Singlepoint. Both are excellent, however, and very quick to use.

Other dot scopes create an electronic dot that is superimposed in the shooter's view through the scope. The catch with these is that the user needs to replace the batteries from time to time, making them hard to store. Also, unlike dot scopes which use available light, the electronic dot scopes have to be adjusted manually to make the dot match the environment in which it's being used. This can be a problem during a partly cloudy day or when moving through heavily wooded areas where the amount of light may vary a lot.

Electric dot scopes do have some advantages, however,

since they don't operate on the occluded eye principle. Unlike the Armson O.E.G. or Singlepoint, the electric scopes can be used like a standard scope.

Another plus with the electric scopes is that they can be used at night as well as during the day. The catch is that the eye sees better "from the corners" at night due to the arrangement of cone and rod cells in the retina. Thus, when you look straight at something to see the dot, the object often vanishes in low-light conditions! When you look at the target from an angle, the target appears and the dot vanishes! Can't win. Nighttime use of electric dot scopes isn't as easy as one might expect.

Electric scopes do help out in twilight shooting, however, and often have a slight edge on the available light scopes in this area. The two best-known brands of these scopes available for the Mini-14 are the Aimpoint ($180) and the "Tascorama" or "Battery Dot" Sight from Tasco ($239). These sights use a small battery that powers them for up to thousands of hours and the dot brightness can be adjusted with a manually controlled rheostat.

A new electric dot sighting system, the Elbit Falcon, is just hitting the American market at the time of this writing. Though the Israeli-designed unit was originally made for the AR-15 and Galil rifles, it can be adapted to Weaver scope bases and used on a Mini-14 as easily as a standard scope. The Falcon system doesn't use a tube and has its lens mounted in a high position to allow the use of both eyes when sighting in on a target. Like the Aimpoint and Tasco systems, the Elbit unit uses a small rheostat to adjust the brightness of the dot. Currently, the Falcon is being distributed in the U.S. by ADCO International.

A rather interesting rifle scope with standard cross hairs and an electric dot which can be turned on when needed is the Bushnell Banner "Lite-Site." This offers the best of both types of scopes and is a consideration for those who want the quickness and low-light use of a dot coupled with the long-range accuracy of a reticle sight. Several companies are also approaching the problem of twilight shooting from a slightly different angle by allowing the shooter to switch on a battery-powered unit inside the scope which illuminates the cross hairs.

Care must be taken with any of these systems since they tend to encourage shooters to shoot at targets which can't be seen clearly; great care must be taken to be sure that the bullet won't be dangerous if the target is missed and—of course—the hunter should be certain of what his target really is.

In combat, where quick shooting is often important, the dot scopes and one-power scopes are hard to beat. Scopes which offer magnification—except for sniper work—usually aren't as good as iron sights in combat. Iron sights get on target more quickly and are also less apt to be damaged. Iron sights are also often nearly as fast as dot scopes and much less expensive. Given the expense and fragile nature of all types of scopes, iron sights may be the best bet for the Mini-14 in combat and many other situations.

Probably the fastest method of combat shooting is the "aim point" or "quick kill" method which was perfected by the U.S. military during the Vietnam War. One excellent way of developing this skill is to practice with a BB rifle; the rifle sights aren't used. Rather, both eyes are kept open and targets shot at in a manner used by trap shooters. While this method of shooting isn't of use for target shooting or engaging long-range targets, it can be quick and deadly at close combat ranges.

SILENCERS

"Silencers with regular 5.56 ammunition are a joke," one manufacturer of such equipment once told me. Much of the time this is certainly true. The supersonic crack of the bullet makes it impossible to hide its use with a silencer and the silencer tube itself makes the Mini-14 unwieldy. But a silencer ("sound suppressor" to the purists) on a rifle does make it harder to locate and can also reduce recoil barrel jump.

There are a number of excellent books on silencers; anyone interested in purchasing a silencer should read up on the device before shelling out a lot of money plus $200 tax. One of the best "starter" books is J. David Truby's *Silencers in the 1980s* (available from Paladin Press). Truby gives an excellent overview of the types of silencers available as well as the names and addresses of major manufacturers.

Paladin also offers a number of other good books on silencers including *The Mini-14 Exotic Weapons System,* which has machinist drawings and plans for constructing a silencer (as well as a trip lever for selective-fire conversion).

Jonathan Arthur Ciener, Inc., is one of the best sources of silencers if you decide you need such an accessory.

SLINGS

Slings often aren't needed or may even be a hindrance in combat or when varminting, but they are of use with many other types of shooting situations. Therefore, quick-detach slings should be considered (as should not using a sling).

The best and some of the most reasonably-priced slings are made by Uncle Mike's. Their models cover a wide range of styles from basket-weave leather Cobra Strap to inexpensive nylon slings in camouflage, brown, black, and white for use in snow. Nylon slings come with padded "shoulder savers" or as regular straps; their "Quick-Adjust" sling can be quickly shortened on the rifle so that it doesn't hang in the way when you don't need it.

STOCKS

Many shooters buy the Mini-14 because its traditional stock blends in with other hunting rifles. Other owners of the rifle either like the extra control of a pistol grip or want a combat-style weapon.

If you like the look of wood but want a folding stock, the Ruger folding stock (which is now available to the general public) is a good choice. It can be purchased when the weapon is bought.

Ram-Line also makes a Ruger-style folding stock look-alike on special order. However, these are so similar that most owners of the Mini-14 may just wish to purchase the Ruger stock up front and save a little money.

However, the wood in either of these stocks is not without its faults; it swells with moisture and may change the zero of the rifle or create other problems, and it tends to show nicks and scratches that plastic stocks hide. Therefore, a lot of shooters prefer the new plastic stocks being offered for the Mini-14 by companies other than Ruger.

One major company that produces good folding stocks for the Mini-14 is Choate Machine and Tool. Especially notable are their Zytel (glass-embedded nylon) stocks. These often improve accuracy as well as give the user the popular pistol-grip configuration.

Many users prefer the Choate folding stock over the Ruger since the butt plate doesn't have to be locked open in a separate action. The stock locks in both the closed and open position and is released by depressing a button just above the pistol grip. The metal stock is covered with plastic, which is especially helpful in the very cold, or hot sunshine. The butt of the folder sports a one-inch rubber pad and also has sling swivels at the top of the stock above the pistol grip as well as at the base of the pistol grip to allow a wide range of carrying modes. The Choate folding stock retails for $67.95. Two finishes are available, blued metal and "Nitex," which matches Sturm, Ruger's stainless steel finish.

In an effort to capture the low range of the stock market, Choate also manufactures a folder made of ABS plastic with a plastic rather than rubber butt. While this budget stock is not as tough as their Zytel models, it is far from fragile and the price is only $49.

Choate also makes a full-length plastic stock called the "E2" due to the off-hand notch in the butt which is similar to that of the M14E2 stock. This is especially

When Sturm, Ruger limited sales of their folding-stock Mini-14s to military and police orders, Ram-Line offered a close copy, which Ram-Line continues to sell on a custom basis. Photo courtesy of Ram-Line.

The Choate stock locks in both the closed and open position and is released by depressing a button on the top of the stock just above the pistol grip. Also shown are the Choate bayonet mount for the AR-15 bayonets, and a Choate flash suppressor. Photo courtesy of Choate Machine and Tool.

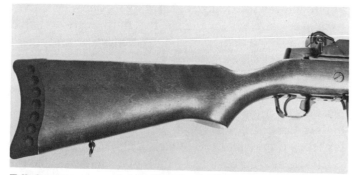

Tall shooters may extend the length of pull for the Mini-14 with the Choate extended butt pad which adds one inch of pull to the standard stock. Photo courtesy of Choate Machine and Tool.

Choate's E2 stock is ideal for use with a bipod as it allows the Mini-14 to be held tightly against the shoulder. Shown is the standard Mini-14 with 30-round magazine, Wooley Burger bipod, and Choate flash suppressor. Photo courtesy of Choate Machine and Tool.

Ram-Line's Zytel plastic folding stock is the ideal lightweight folder. Also shown on this standard Mini-14 are the Ram-Line bipod and Combo Mag. Photo courtesy of Ram-Line.

Choate offers a traditionally-styled Zytel plastic stock for those who prefer a weather- and humidity-proof stock, but shy from the modern skeletal butt stocks and metallic stocks. Shown is the stainless steel Mini-14 with a Choate Nitex-finished AR-15-style flash suppressor. Photo courtesy of Choate Machine and Tool.

useful for those who wish to use a bipod, as it allows the Mini-14 to be held tightly against the shoulder. The stock is skeletonized to keep its weight down while maintaining strength and rigidity. The stock also has a rubber butt pad; while the recoil of the .223 doesn't warrant a recoil pad, the rubber does help keep the stock in place when shouldered. All in all, the E2 stock is of excellent design and is available from Choate for $44.95.

All three types of stocks can be ordered directly from Choate or from a number of other companies and dealers who carry Choate products. For extra-tall shooters, Choate also offers an extended butt pad that adds one inch to the length of pull for $15. The company also offers a ventilated fiberglass handguard to upgrade older Mini-14s with the wooden handguard.

Ram-Line also makes a unique folding stock that should be considered by those wanting a folding stock that is lightweight. The Ram-Line folder is all plastic and weighs about half as much as most metal and plastic folding stocks. This tough Zytel stock also has the "Laser" pistol grip which Ram-Line originally designed for the AR-15. This pistol grip has a finger swell which allows for a firmer hold; it also has a sliding plate on the base so that a small storage compartment is available for carrying odds and ends. Cost for the lightweight Ram-Line stock is $62.50.

For those looking toward the future, a "K-3 Bullpup" kit is offered by Westminister Arms. The stock covers the factory trigger/safety; double rods connect the pistol grip trigger to the enclosed trigger. It is important to note that the safety is mounted behind the new trigger and is not quite as safe as the Ruger safety. Also, the unit should not be fired from the left shoulder because the operating rod and/or the ejected case can cause injuries. A cheek pad is mounted in the old rear-sight assembly and a new rear sight/carrying handle which looks like that of the AR-15 and can use AR-15 scope mounts replaces the upper half of the handguard. A raised AR-15-style front sight clamps onto the rifle's barrel. Cost for the whole kit is $190. Unfortunately, early Westminister K-3 bullpup stocks

The "K–3 Bullpup" stock kit, offered by Westminister Arms, covers the rifle's factory trigger/safety assembly and double rods connect the pistol grip trigger to the rifle's original trigger. The safety is located behind the new trigger, a cheek pad is mounted in the old rear sight assembly, and a new rear sight/carrying handle replace the upper half of the handguard. A raised AR-15-style front sight clamps securely onto the rifle's barrel. Photo courtesy of Westminister Arms.

weren't as strong as might be hoped for and fitted rather poorly. Currently, Westminister is working to correct these problems and is planning on marketing a "military grade" stock.

More traditional plastic stocks are also available for those Mini-14 owners who like the idea of a weather- and humidity-proof stock but dislike the "spacey" look of pistol grips. One is manufactured by Mitchell Arms, Inc., for $70; the stock is actually stronger and lighter than the wooden stock but black and a bit longer with its recoil pad. Choate also makes a traditional-style Zytel stock for $47.

To change over to any of these stocks, it is necessary to remove the internal metal parts of the original Ruger stock (see step 24 in the disassembly section of this book) and place the parts in the new stock.

* * *

The Mini-14 is a handy, affordable rifle that is capable of being modified for combat or used as a sporter. The right accessories and modifications can greatly improve it and the wrong ones can greatly degrade its potential.

Become familiar with your equipment so you can operate it well. Get only what you need and practice.

Practice.

Practice.

Appendix:

Manufacturers, Distributors, and Publishers

MANUFACTURERS

Iver Johnson
2202 Redmond Rd.
Jacksonville, AR 72076
> (Manufacturers of M-1 Carbine chambered for .30 Carbine, 9mm Luger, 5.7mm Johnson, and .22 LR)

Springfield Armory
111 E. Exchange St.
Geneseo, IL 61254
> (Manufacturer/distributor of M1A, M14, M1A-A1, M1 Garand, M1 "Tanker Garand," Beretta BM-59, BM-59 Alpine Trooper, BM-59 Nigerian model; semiauto and selective-fire models of most are available)

Sturm, Ruger, & Co.
Southport, CT 06490
> (Manufacturers of Mini-14, M14 rifles)

Universal Firearms
3740 E. 10th Ct.
Hialeah, FL 33013
> (Manufacturers of semiauto M1 .30 Carbines and pistols)

ACCESSORIES AND CUSTOM MODIFICATIONS

Accuracy Rifle Systems
P.O. Box 6529
Odessa, TX 79767-6529
    (Rebarreling, accuracy work for Mini-14 rifles)

ADCO International
1 Wyman St.
Woburn, MA 01801
    (Distributor of Elbit Falcon electric dot-aiming system)

Aimpoint USA
201 Elden St., Suite 302
Herndon, VA 22070
    (Aimpoint scopes)

Alpha Armament
105 E. Main St.
Lebanon, OH 45036
    (AK-74 style muzzle brake)

Armson
P.O. Box 2130
Farmington Hills, MI 48018
    (Armson O.E.G. available-light dot scope)

Assault Systems
869 Horan Dr.
St. Louis, MO 63026
    (Rifle cases and accessories)

Beeman Precision Arms
47 Paul Dr.
San Rafael, CA 94903
    (SS-1 and SS-2 scopes and other accessories)

Brigade Quartermasters, Ltd.
1025 Cobb International Blvd.
Kennesaw, GA 30144-4349
    (Military surplus-style equipment and accessories)

B-Square Company
Box 11281
Fort Worth, TX 76109
> (Scope mounts for most Mini-14s)

Bushnell Optical Co.
2828 E. Foothill Blvd.
Pasadena, CA 91107
> (Banner and other model scopes for Mini-14 and M14 rifles)

Cherokee Gun Accessories
830 Woodside Rd.
Redwood, CA 94061
> (Cheekpieces for use with scope)

Choate Machine and Tool Company
Box 218
Bald Knob, AR 72010
> (Manufacturer of wide range of stocks, flash suppressors, handguards, etc., for Mini-14)

D & E Magazine Mfg.
P.O. Box 4876
Sylmar, CA 91342
> (Extended magazines for Mini-14)

D. C. Brennan Firearms, Inc.
P.O. Box 2732
Cincinnati, OH 45201
> (Nil-Flash flash suppressors for Mini-14)

Defense Moulding Enterprises, Inc.
Box 4328
Carson, CA 90745
> (Plastic magazines for Mini-14)

E & L Manufacturing
Star Rt. 1, Box 569, Schoolhouse Rd.
Cave Creek, AZ 85331
> (Rigid brass catchers and barrel shrouds for Mini-14)

Excalibur Enterprises
P.O. Box 266
Emmaus, PA 18049
(Night-vision equipment)

Executive Protection Products, Inc.
1834 First St., Ste. E
Napa, CA 94559
(Laser-sighting systems)

Fabian Brothers Sporting Goods, Inc.
1510 Morena Blvd., Suite G
San Diego, CA 92110
(DTA Mil/Brake muzzle compensator for Mini-14 or M14)

Feather Enterprises
2500 Central Ave.
Boulder, CO 80301
(Accessories for the Mini-14)

Fiber Pro
P.O. Box 83732
San Diego, CA 92138
(Fiberglass and composite stocks for M14, M1A, Mini-14, and other rifles)

Harris Engineering
Barlow, KY 42024
(Harris bipod)

Harry Owen
P.O. Box 5337
Hacienda Heights, CA 91745
(Cartridge adapters for using different types of .22 rimfire ammunition in the Mini-14)

Hydra Systems
Box 3461
Bridgeport, CT 06605
(Laser-sighting systems)

I & I, Enterprises
6828 Platt Ave.
Canoga Park, CA 91304
   (Mini-14 firing pins)

JFS, Inc.
P.O. Box 12204
Salem, OR 97309
   (Manufacturer of Redi-Mag)

Jonathan Arthur Ciener, Inc.
6850 Riverside Dr.
Titusville, FL 32780
   (Manufacturer of Mini-14 .22LR conversion kit;
   automatic firearms; silencers)

Laser Arms Corp.
P.O. Box 4647
Las Vegas, NV 89127
   (Laser-sighting systems)

Laser Products
18285 Mt. Baldy Circle
Fountain Valley, CA 92708
   (Laser-aiming system for Mini-14)

Light Enterprises
P.O. Box 3811
Littleton, CO 80161
   (Nightsighter night sight)

Michaels of Oregon ("Uncle Mike's")
P.O. Box 13010
Portland, OR 97213
   (Rifle slings, scope covers, detachable sling swivels)

Military Surplus Supply
5594 Airways
Memphis, TN 38116
   (Camo covers for firearms)

Millett Sights
16131 Gothard
Huntington Beach, CA 92647
(Replacement rear sights for standard Mini-14)

Mitchell Arms
19007 South Reyes Ave.
Compton, CA 90221
(Manufacturer of Mini-14 plastic stock)

Newman's GI Supply
RR #1, Box 782
Augusta, NJ 07822
(Combat support vests, military surplus gear)

Numrich Arms Corporation
West Hurley, NY 12491
(Mini-14 parts)

Parellex Corporation
1090 Fargo
Elk Grove Village, IL 60007
(Distributor of magazines, flash suppressors, slings, cases, scope mounts, etc.)

Ram-Line, Inc.
406 Violet St.
Golden, CO 80401
(Manufacturer of AR-15/Mini-14 combo mag, Mini-14 accessories including plastic folding stock)

Sherwood International
18714 Parthenia St.
Northridge, CA 91324
(Distributor of magazines, bayonets, slings, cases, etc.)

Sierra Supply
P.O. Box 1390
Durango, CO 81301
(Cleaning equipment, Break-Free CLP, and military ammunition/magazine carrying pouches and other surplus equipment)